Financial
Shenanigans

Financial Shenanigans

How to Detect Accounting Gimmicks and Fraud in Financial Reports

Howard M. Schilit, Ph.D., CPA

McGraw-Hill, Inc.
New York   St. Louis   San Francisco   Auckland   Bogotá
Caracas   Lisbon   London   Madrid   Mexico City   Milan
Montreal   New Delhi   San Juan   Singapore
Sydney   Tokyo   Toronto

Library of Congress Cataloging-in-Publication Data

Schilit, Howard Mark, date.
   Financial shenanigans : how to detect acconting gimmicks and
fraud in financial reports / Howard M. Schilit.
       p.   cm.
   Includes bibliographical references and index.
   ISBN 0-07-056131-1
   1. Financial statements, misleading. 2. Fraud. I. Title.
HF5681.B2S3243 1993
657′.3—dc20   93–6481
                                         CIP

ISBN   0-07-056131-1

 3 4 5 6 7 8 9 10 11 12 13 14 BKMBKM 9 9 8 7 6 5 4

*The sponsoring editor for this book was Caroline Carney, the editing supervi-
sor was Olive H. Collen, and the production supervisor was Pamela A. Pelton.
The book was set in Palatino by McGraw-Hill's Professional Book Group composition unit.*

This book is printed on recycled, acid-free paper
containing a minimum of 50% recycled de-inked
fiber.

Dedication

Twenty years ago I was introduced to the writings of Dr. Abraham J. Briloff, a scholar and professor of accounting at CUNY-Baruch in New York. Professor Briloff, a vocal critic of misleading financial reports, became a leading spokesman against "shenanigans" in financial statements. His books on this subject, entitled *Unaccountable Accounting* (1972), *More Debits than Credits* (1976), and *The Truth about Corporate Accounting* (1981), alerted us to the substantial flexibility that management has in reporting its financial results and of the financial shenanigans that managers can and do use in manipulating their companies' financial statements. In the acknowledgments to *The Truth about Corporate Accounting*, Briloff aroused my interest in continuing his work when he stated:

> I want here and now to express my appreciation to those who, in academe or practice, may, from my writings, recognize the exhilaration and intellectual stimulation that may be derived from investigative writing in the realm of accountancy, or economics generally, and who thereupon undertake its pursuit.

A second major influence shaping my thinking about accounting tricks was my outstanding professor at SUNY-Binghamton in New York, Philip M. Piaker. Professor Piaker, also a Briloff disciple, not only taught me the basic skills needed to read and evaluate financial reports but also helped foster my intellectual skills and the curiosity necessary to question and challenge commonly held assumptions in financial reporting.

Contents

Preface

If the Food and Drug Administration rather than the Securities and Exchange Commission (SEC) regulated financial reporting, you might see this warning on each financial report: BEWARE: RELYING ON THIS REPORT COULD BE HAZARDOUS TO YOUR WEALTH. This label would alert investors and lenders to the substantial risks of relying on financial reports, whether audited or not. For example, such reports may fail to alert investors and lenders to a company's actual or imminent financial difficulties; they may fail to measure a company's actual financial performance and its economic condition accurately; or they may simply be incomplete.

Since it is unlikely that such a governmental warning will appear on financial statements any time soon, investors and lenders themselves must remain alert to the possibility of deficiencies, or face the risk of making misinformed decisions on the basis of deliberately incomplete or misleading data. By relying on such data, for example, investors may be more prone to buying stock in losing companies, and bankers more prone to lending money to overly risky ones.

Anyone who reads and relies on financial reports knows that deciphering the "true" economic story can be daunting, even for experienced analysts. At times, management makes it more difficult for investors and lenders by using accounting tricks, or "shenanigans," in financial reports. So how can investors and others who rely on such reports have confidence that the reports are complete and truthful? How can *you* be confident that management is not using accounting gimmicks to boost anemic earnings or to smooth out erratic earnings?

In performing postmortems on scores of successful companies that suddenly failed—including Crazy Eddie, W.T. Grant, and Regina Company—I have often been able to identify signs of accounting gimmicks in financial reports. Unfortunately, few investors, analysts, or bankers are familiar with these signs; as a result, they often fail to notice them in time. Sadly, their failure to detect artificially inflated assets or income (two common types of shenanigans) often leads investors and lenders to take needless risks.

Seven Major Shenanigans

The seven shenanigans described in this book all enable management to manipulate net income. The first five boost current-year profits; the last two shift current-year profits to the future. The seven shenanigans are:

1. Recording revenue before it is earned
2. Creating fictitious revenue
3. Boosting profits with nonrecurring transactions
4. Shifting current expenses to a later period
5. Failing to record or disclose liabilities
6. Shifting current income to a later period
7. Shifting future expenses to an earlier period

These shenanigans, and the corporate vignettes used in this book to illustrate them, were compiled from many sources, including a review of the financial statements of companies that failed, were sanctioned by the SEC, or were sanctioned by the courts.

What Are the Objective and Message of This Book?

This book has two simple objectives:

- To improve the quality of financial analysis by helping investors and lenders find shenanigans, or accounting tricks, in financial reports

- To improve the quality of financial reporting by illustrating some common transgressions that have allowed companies to enjoy short-term gain—often at the expense of dramatic long-term pain

The message of *Financial Shenanigans* is *not* that most companies and accountants "cook the books." On the contrary, shenanigans are the exception, not the rule. However, an investor or a banker must maintain a healthy skepticism in order to make prudent economic decisions.

Shenanigans can occur in companies of any size, public or private, young or old. By knowing what they are and how to find them, readers will be able to evaluate the performance and value of any company far more accurately.

Who Will Benefit from Reading This Book?

While this book is intended primarily to help those who read and interpret financial statements (i.e., investors and lenders) to make better decisions, *Financial Shenanigans* will also be valuable to auditors, corporate managers, insurers, attorneys, financial regulators, and business professors and their students.

Methodology: Lessons Learned from Financial Reporting Failures

Many people believe that the best training for professionals (including investors, lenders, and CPAs) is to be immersed in actual case studies involving ethical conflicts. For example, Robert J. Sack, former chief accountant of the Division of Enforcement at the SEC, emphasized the importance of using actual case studies of SEC enforcement actions or court proceedings in teaching about financial shenanigans. He compared this case approach with the training of medical students, stating:

> It seems to me that there is a close analogy between the education of a medical doctor and the education of a professional

accountant. [The] objective of a medical autopsy is simply to learn what went wrong, and to make a judgment as to what might have been done differently. The medical profession tries to learn from those failures, to expand its list of answers. Unfortunately, the financial reporting process sometimes fails too.... We must find a way for accountants to use those financial reporting failures in the expansion of our knowledge base.

This book uses such an approach, examining court cases and SEC enforcement proceedings against companies that filed false and misleading financial statements. And those lessons can serve as a checklist of tactics to watch for in evaluating financial statements today.

Illustrations in this book pertain to public companies and were obtained from public sources (mainly SEC enforcement actions, news clippings, and court records). While the illustrations are from public companies, the lessons taught are equally applicable in evaluating any company, whether public or privately held. In fact, since financial statements of private companies are generally not audited, they are even more susceptible to financial shenanigans.

By following specific recommendations, readers will not only develop a healthy skepticism when reading financial statements, they will also make better economic decisions. Specifically, investors will learn to identify overvalued companies and will consequently pick winning stocks more often; bankers and other lenders will learn to spot companies with weak cash flows and unrecorded liabilities, enabling them to lend money more judiciously to such risky entities; and managers of companies that file misleading financial reports will learn that they not only hurt those outside the company who rely on these reports but also injure the companies themselves.

A Note about the Companies Cited in Financial Shenanigans

The corporate vignettes that appear in this book are intended solely to illustrate applications (and misapplications) of accounting principles. Some of the improprieties cited occurred several years ago and, in many cases, under managers and executives who are no longer associated with the respective companies.

International Network of Financial Shenanigans Busters

For those readers who not only want to detect financial shenanigans but who also want to help eliminate them, I am launching a new international organization. This new organization will serve as a clearinghouse and network: not only disseminating ideas and techniques for detecting shenanigans but also bringing together people who can help one another in preventing, detecting, and remedying misleading information and fraud in financial reports. For more information about membership in the association, please write or call:

HOWARD M. SCHILIT
Center for Financial Research and Analysis
10800 Mazwood Place
Rockville, MD 20852
(301) 530-8224

Acknowledgments

This book benefited from the insights of many wonderful people who share my goal of eliminating financial shenanigans. To them I am truly grateful: Dr. Ajay Adhikari (The American University), Dr. Leopold Bernstein (CUNY-Baruch), Dr. Abraham Briloff (CUNY-Baruch), Charles Crawford (London Manhattan Company), Sam Dedio (Standard & Poor's), Michael Kigin (Securities & Exchange Commission), Charles Landy, Esq. (Medrod, Redman & Gartlan), Bernard Loehr (Eastman Kodak Company), Lorin Luchs (BDO Seidman), Dr. Philip Meyer (Boston University), Phyllis Minott (Eli Lilly Company), Ted O'glove (*Quality of Earnings Report*), Wayne Upton (Financial Accounting Standards Board), and Michael Willner (Federal Filings, Inc.).

The professionals at McGraw-Hill (Caroline Carney and Olive Collen) are to be congratulated for their assistance in shaping the book and providing editorial suggestions.

On a more personal level, I would like to thank my brothers Rob and Warren for their invaluable assistance in developing, shaping, and editing the manuscript. Last, but certainly not least, I want to express my love and appreciation for the support of my wife, Diane, and our three terrific children, Jonathan, Suzanne, and Amy.

1
What Are Shenanigans?

What Are Financial Shenanigans?

In a 1964 pornography case, the U.S. Supreme Court reviewed a French film, *The Lovers*, to determine whether it violated obscenity laws. After reviewing the film, Justice Potter Stewart was at a loss for words to define obscenity, stating: "It's hard to define but you know it when you see it."

Unlike obscenity, financial shenanigans are easy to define but more difficult to detect in practice. Financial shenanigans are actions or omissions intended to hide or distort the real financial performance or financial condition of an entity. They range from minor deceptions (such as failing to clearly segregate operating from nonoperating gains and losses) to more serious misapplications of accounting principles (such as failing to write off worthless assets; they also include fraudulent behavior, such as the recording of fictitious revenue to overstate the real financial performance). Since management is clever about hiding its tricks, investors and others must be alert for signs of shenanigans.

THE SEVEN SHENANIGANS

Shenanigan No. 1: Recording Revenue Too Soon

1. Shipping goods before a sale is finalized
2. Recording revenue when important uncertainties exist
3. Recording revenue when future services are still due

Shenanigan No. 2: Recording Bogus Revenues

1. Recording income on the exchange of similar assets
2. Recording refunds from suppliers as revenue
3. Using bogus estimates on interim financial reports

Shenanigan No. 3: Boosting Income with One-Time Gains

1. Boosting profits by selling undervalued assets
2. Boosting profits by retiring debt
3. Failing to segregate unusual and nonrecurring gains or losses from recurring income
4. Burying losses under noncontinuing operations

Shenanigan No. 4: Shifting Current Expenses to a Later Period

1. Improperly capitalizing costs
2. Depreciating or amortizing costs too slowly
3. Failing to write off worthless assets

Shenanigan No. 5: Failing to Record or Disclose All Liabilities

1. Reporting revenue rather than a liability when cash is received
2. Failing to accrue expected or contingent liabilities
3. Failing to disclose commitments and contingencies
4. Engaging in transactions to keep debt off the books

Shenanigan No. 6: Shifting Current Income to a Later Period

1. Creating reserves to shift sales revenue to a later period

Shenanigan No. 7: Shifting Future Expenses to the Current Period

1. Accelerating discretionary expenses into the current period
2. Writing off future years' depreciation or amortization

Why Do Shenanigans Exist?

While most people agree that gimmicks can distort financial statements, there are many theories on the causes. Based on my research, there are three general reasons for shenanigans: (1) It pays to do it, (2) it's easy to do, and (3) it's unlikely you'll get caught.

It Pays to Do It

Some managers will resort to accounting gimmicks if they are personally enriched by doing so. Thus, when bonuses encourage managers to post higher sales and profits (with no questions asked about how those gains were achieved), an incentive for using shenanigans can be created. Unfortunately, misguided incentive plans are not uncommon today in corporations.

In explaining why companies use financial shenanigans to manage earnings, Professor Abraham Briloff remarked:

> ...because it's their report card. Executives like their bonuses and the other perquisites that are tied to reported earnings.

Be Alert for Misguided Management Incentives. Like most of us, management's behavior is affected by rewards and punishments. Since many companies offer bonuses and stock options based on financial statement measures, executives and managers are motivated to report more favorable financial results. Similarly, if underperforming divisions in companies are threatened with layoffs or lower compensation for their managers, those managers will often search for ways to report stronger results. Because of pressure to report higher sales and higher profits, managers may be creative in their interpretation of Generally Accepted Accounting Principles (GAAP) to help them report stronger financial results.

Consider what happened at Matrix Science Corporation. According to the SEC, management set sales growth targets that apparently were difficult to reach in 1985. Feeling pressure to meet those targets, managers engaged in several shenanigans (characterized by the SEC as fraud) to achieve those goals, including: (1) keeping financial quarters "open" beyond the last day of a quarter to record additional sales revenues, (2) preprinting invoices for orders that had not been shipped, and (3) delaying the issuance of credit memoranda on a timely basis for orders that had been returned.

Companies such as Matrix Science, which break the law or breach accepted accounting standards, provide the most colorful and noteworthy examples of financial shenanigans. Yet it is the other, not-so-obvious (and far more common) shenanigans that are most worrisome, because they use the appearance of propriety to keep the investor's guard down.

Company Profile

Matrix Science Corporation

Matrix Science, apparently motivated by misguided management incentives, used a variety of fraudulent techniques to boost sales—and boost managers' bonuses.

Matrix Science designed, manufactured, and sold electrical connectors for use in aircraft, ground radar, and other electronics and communications applications. In August 1987, the SEC staff contacted the company regarding an investigation of its allegedly fraudulent financial reports. Matrix Science's board then voted to suspend the president and chief executive officer. The company's fortunes declined rapidly, and several years later, a slimmed-down Matrix Science was sold to AMP Corporation. See Fig. 1-1.

A compensation structure that overemphasizes the bottom line provides an environment that sometimes encourages the types of shenanigans used at Matrix Science Corporation. Professor Paul Healy of MIT undertook a study to show empirically that management benefited by choosing accounting procedures that produced higher earnings. Healy found a connection between bonus schemes and the accounting choices that executives made. Specifically, he noted that executives whose bonuses already rewarded them up to a ceiling tended to choose accounting options that minimized reported profits, while those whose plans had no ceiling chose profit-boosting options. Thus, if no additional bonus is paid once profits reach a certain level, it is no longer in the executive's interest for reported profits to exceed that amount. In such

Matrix Science Corporation
Stock Price Movement 1984–1988

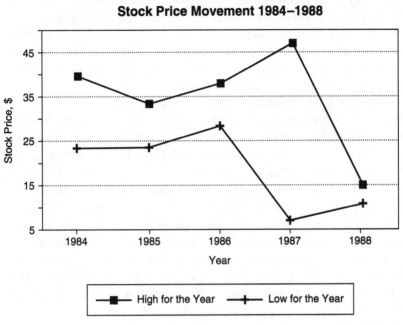

Fig. 1-1.

Matrix Science Corporation

	Price	
Year	High	Low
1984	$38.75	$23.25
1985	$33.00	$23.50
1986	$38.00	$28.50
1987	$47.00	$ 6.50
1988	$15.25	$10.75
1989	Not Traded	
1990	Not Traded	

cases, the manager would be better off deferring any profits above the maximum bonus level until they were needed in the future to sustain the manager's own income.

It's Easy to Do It.

Managers select accounting methods (i.e., inventory valuation or amortization of intangible assets) from a variety of acceptable choices. Thus, depending on the methods selected and the numerous estimates that must be made, a company's reported profit could vary considerably and yet still be in compliance with GAAP.

With many choices and judgments required, honest managers grapple with such decisions with the goal of finding accounting policies that portray fairly the company's financial performance. Unscrupulous managers, unfortunately, use the flexibility in GAAP to distort the financial reports.

Indeed, it is surprisingly easy for managers to use accounting gimmicks to manipulate financial statements. This is true for various reasons, including the following: (1) There is substantial flexibility in interpreting GAAP, (2) GAAP can be applied to boost a company's reported profits, and (3) changes in GAAP by the Financial Accounting Standards Board (FASB) often occur long after a deficiency in financial reporting becomes evident.

Unlike tax legislation and the related Treasury Department Regulations, financial accounting standards are fairly broad and consequently allow management considerable flexibility in interpreting them. Thus, decisions on whether to capitalize a cost or expense it—or on selecting amortization periods for fixed assets—depend on management judgment.

Furthermore, management can structure transactions, or decide when and how to implement new accounting rules, to maximize its reporting goals. The use of stock compensation plans (which produce no change in income) as a substitute for other forms of compensation has grown increasingly popular at many corporations. Similarly, companies can structure lease agreements to keep the debt off their books (e.g., using an operating lease approach). And today companies have various alternatives concerning how and when to record postretirement costs [*Statement of Financial Accounting Standards (SFAS) No. 106*].

Question Overly Liberal Accounting Rules. Because management has substantial control over the numbers reported, consider whether the accounting policies selected are overly aggressive. Consider various accounting policies of a company, such as inventory method, amortization period, and revenue recognition policy. Further, consider any changes in accounting policies and the reasons cited for them.

Beyond the realm of ethics, judgment plays an especially important role in the banking and insurance industries. Bankers use judgment in determining whether and when to write off loans that may fail. If they are slow to recognize problem loans and fail to write them off, the bank will continue accruing interest on shaky loans. The result on the bank's financial statements is an overstatement of assets, interest income, and profits.

Watch for Poor Internal Controls. Besides utilizing the flexibility of GAAP, management may have little difficulty distorting financial reports if the company has weak internal controls. Such controls relate to the organizational structure and to corporate procedures for safeguarding assets against losses and for ensuring the reliability of financial records for external reporting purposes. Strong controls (i.e., checks and balances) tend to reduce the temptation for management to engage in shenanigans. If safeguards and controls are lacking, however, unethical employees may engage in shenanigans with impunity. While independent auditors scrutinize the adequacy of these controls, it may be difficult for readers of financial statements to ascertain whether the controls contain weaknesses.

It's Unlikely You'll Get Caught

Just as some people cheat on their tax returns because they think they won't get caught by the IRS, companies may use accounting tricks because they believe that they won't get caught by auditors or regulators. Unfortunately, for the reasons outlined below, they are usually right.

Quarterly Financial Statements Are Unaudited. Investors and bankers who rely on quarterly financial statements and press releases of financial performance may believe that those reports have the blessing of an independent CPA. Unfortunately, that's not usually true. Only annual financial statements of publicly held companies must be audited; quarterly statements need not be. Moreover, since most companies are privately held, they are rarely audited by an outside CPA. Consequently, when companies use accounting tricks on unaudited financial statements, there is little risk that they will be caught. As a result, investors must be especially careful when reading quarterly financial statements.

Here's one example of tricks in quarterly reports. Investors in a North Carolina builder of prefabricated homes, Manufactured Homes, learned the hard way about the pitfalls of relying on an unaudited quarterly report (Form 10-Q; see Chapter 2). During the first nine months of 1987, the company posted a pretax profit of $10.6 million on sales of $148 million. But in the fourth quarter, the company abruptly recorded an $8.5 million loss reserve for credit sales, wiping out those earlier gains and resulting in only a small profit for the year. Why the big surprise in the fourth quarter? Apparently, the company had been understating its potential credit losses all along. That was the conclusion of Peat Marwick Main & Co. (now called KPMG Peat Marwick), its independent auditors. In fact, Peat had earlier urged management to increase the loss reserves. Management resisted and got its way, because quarterly Form 10-Qs do not require auditor approval. In the fourth quarter, however, the company had to bite the bullet and comply with the auditors' position by writing off the loss reserves. According to Peat partner (and former chief accountant of the SEC's Division of Enforcement) Glenn Perry, "If we had a requirement to formally review quarterly data, we wouldn't have had a surprise fourth-quarter adjustment."

Company Profile

Manufactured Homes, Inc.

Manufactured Homes, Inc., was charged with overstating profits on its unaudited quarterly financial statements.

Manufactured Homes builds and sells prefab, low-priced, single-family homes. The SEC charged that the company's financial statements for the years 1986–1988 were misleading, resulting in an inflated stock price. Since that time, the company's fortunes plummeted; it reported 1990 annual revenue of $28 million, representing a rapid decline over the preceding three years. Manufactured Homes, whose market value approached $80 million in 1987, filed for bankruptcy in July 1991. See Fig. 1-2.

Partly because of misleading information in 10-Qs, some observers have questioned whether quarterly reports should

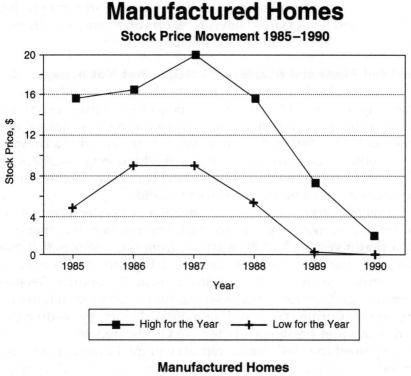

Manufactured Homes
Stock Price Movement 1985–1990

Fig. 1-2.

Manufactured Homes

Year	Price High	Low
1985	$15.50	$4.50
1986	$16.50	$8.88
1987	$20.00	$8.88
1988	$15.75	$5.25
1989	$ 7.38	$0.25
1990	$ 2.00	$0.06

even be required. For example, 1992 Democratic presidential candidate Paul Tsongas argued that these reports are unaudited and that management becomes overly focused on maximizing short-term results at the expense of the long term. Further, he pointed out that our major competitors, Japan and Germany, require only annual financial statements. Moreover, even SEC Commissioner Edward Fleishman questioned the value of quarterly reports. Notwithstanding the positions of Messrs. Tsongas and Fleishman that some managers become overly focused on short-term profits, investors and lenders need interim reports on a company's financial progress, and the 10-Q meets that need.

Audited Financial Statements Help ...but Not Always. By now you probably have some doubts about the truthfulness of quarterly reports, but you may still be confident that the annual audited financial statements will give you the true story. Generally they will; but they too may fail to warn you that a company is about to go belly up. Consider the following examples of Chrysler Corporation and United American Bank, about which investors received no warning from the auditors.

Chrysler Corporation. We all remember Chrysler teetering on the brink of bankruptcy a decade ago. The untold part of that story is that investors had no warning from the auditors that the company was almost out of business. Chrysler's auditors gave the company a clean bill of health in its audit report in 1980— even though Chrysler's financial condition had been deteriorating rapidly during the preceding months. In fact, by reading the chairman's and president's letter "To Our Shareholders," which accompanied the 1980 annual report, you might never have suspected a problem. In fact, they painted a very rosy picture stating:

> During the year, cash and marketable securities increased from $409 million to $523 million. The company's working capital, its current ratio and its debt-to-equity ratio were the best in five years.

The contents of this letter were at best trivial and more likely misleading. At a time when Chrysler was running out of cash, it tried to give the impression that its liquidity was improving. The sad truth for investors was that Chrysler's liquidity was weak, and the letter from the president should have made that point clear.

United American Bank. On January 28, 1983, Ernst & Whinney (now Ernst & Young) delivered its audit opinion on the 1982 annual report of the United American Bank (UAB) of Knoxville, Tennessee. It had not been a good year for UAB. According to the financial report, the bank posted a $23 million loss and wrote off $9.3 million in bad loans, more than four times as much as in 1981; yet the auditors gave UAB an "unqualified" or "clean" opinion (indicating that no problems existed), rather than a "going concern qualification."

A week after the report was released, the Federal Deposit Insurance Corporation (FDIC) ordered UAB to recall and correct the annual report, which the FDIC said was "materially false and misleading." In response, the bank issued a press release, announcing that it expected additional losses that had come to light during the FDIC's recent examination of its loan portfolio.

That was an understatement, since on February 14—only 17 days after Ernst had delivered a clean opinion—the Tennessee Commissioner of Banking declared UAB insolvent because of heavy loan losses and shut it down.

The question that many investors, lenders, and others asked was: "Where were the accountants?" And UAB was just one of many cases in which the auditor gave a clean opinion of a bank or thrift shortly before it failed. Incredibly, of the 30 thrifts that failed in California in 1985, 28 were given clean opinions the year before they went under. The U.S. General Accounting Office recently studied 11 failed thrifts and found a startling reality gap: Accountants had reported that the S&Ls had a $44 million positive net worth; when the thrifts failed, most within one year of the audit, the S&Ls were $1.5 billion in the hole.

What Types of Companies Are Most Likely To Use Shenanigans?

While it is relatively easy for managers to use shenanigans and there is only a moderate chance of getting caught, *most companies do not* intentionally distort their financial reports. Unfortunately, since you never know in advance which companies do publish misleading information, it is prudent to be a bit suspicious of all and search for early warning signs of problems. Such signs often include (1) a weak control environment (i.e., lack of independent members on the board of directors or lack of a competent/independent external auditor), (2) management facing extreme competitive pressure, and (3) management known or suspected of having questionable character. Be particularly alert for these factors in the following types of companies: fast-growth companies whose real growth is beginning to slow; basket-case companies struggling to survive; newly public companies; and private companies.

The growth of all fast-growth companies will eventually slow considerably. That is when managers might be tempted to use accounting gimmicks. Investors and lenders should be alert to shenanigans in all such companies. At the other extreme, managers of very weak companies might be tempted to use accounting tricks to deceive the outside world into thinking that their problems are minor. Investors and lenders should be particularly alert when a company is in danger of falling out of compliance with bank lending covenants on such financial measures as minimum net worth and working capital. Many newly public companies whose shares are first issued through an initial public offering, or IPO, have never been audited before and may lack strong internal controls. Shenanigans may be prevalent. Finally, private companies—particularly those that are closely held and have not been audited—are more likely to use shenanigans.

How Does the Stock Market React to Shenanigans?

The public assumes and expects that financial statements measure financial transactions accurately. Not surprisingly, when a company is discovered to be "cooking the books," the price of its stock generally declines rapidly and steeply. In fact, it is not uncommon for nothing more than rumors or unproved allegations to send a stock price into a free fall.

Consider the case of fast-growing (ranked no. 2 on *Business Week*'s 1991 list of fastest-growing small companies) Knowledge-Ware, Inc., headed by former Minnesota Vikings quarterback Fran Tarkenton. The first sign of trouble surfaced in May 1991 when seven top executives, including Tarkenton, sold stock valued at $14 million. A bombshell was then dropped in October when shareholders filed class-action suits against Knowledge-Ware and its executives, charging that the company artificially inflated the stock price by recording revenue before it was earned (Shenanigan No. 1, discussed in Chapter 3). Not surprisingly, the stock price dived from a high of $43 in April to $12 in October 1991—a decline of 72 percent.

The sobering news of the stock price decline was mirrored in the company's financial reports for the six months ended December 1991, where KnowledgeWare reported that its incredibly fast growth in revenues had all but come to a screeching halt—up only 2 percent over the previous year. Apparently, this rapid stock price decline occurred in anticipation of weaker operating results. One obvious question: Did real growth start slowing in 1991, or were the previous years' financial reports overstating revenue by using financial shenanigans? That is, perhaps the 1991 report reflects more conservative accounting policies, whereas the previous ones did not.

Company Profile

KnowledgeWare, Inc.

KnowledgeWare's stock price plunged upon news that it may have recorded revenue before it was earned.

KnowledgeWare designs, develops, and markets an integrated line of computer-aided software engineering products. Its annual revenues exceed $100 million and had been growing at better than 107 percent for the last three years. Knowledge-Ware, whose market value in April 1991 exceeded $500 million, was worth approximately $130 million by the middle of 1992. See Fig. 1-3.

And That Is Why We Need Protection

If the financial statements of certain companies contain shenanigans—fraudulent, misleading, and/or incomplete information not detected by auditors or regulators—how can investors and others be protected? Are there signs that investors should look for in reading financial reports that will indicate the information is false? The answers are yes, investors do need protection; and yes, there are signs to look for. Chapter 2 discusses what signs to look for and where to find them.

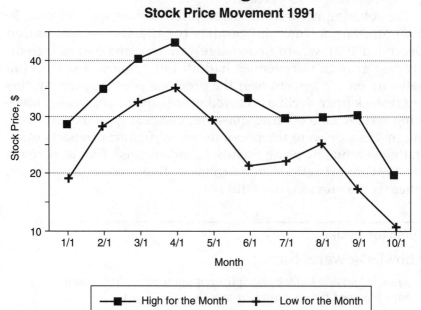

Knowledgeware
Stock Price Movement 1991

Knowledgeware

	Price	
Year	High	Low
1/1	$29.00	$19.25
2/1	$35.00	$28.50
3/1	$40.25	$32.75
4/1	$43.25	$35.00
5/1	$37.00	$29.50
6/1	$33.50	$21.25
7/1	$29.75	$22.00
8/1	$29.75	$25.00
9/1	$30.00	$17.00
10/1	$19.50	$10.50

Fig. 1-3.

2
Searching for Shenanigans

Detection is, or ought to be, an exact science, and should be treated in the same cold and unemotional way.

When you have eliminated the impossible, whatever remains, however improbable, must be the truth.
SIR ARTHUR CONAN DOYLE
author and creator of
Sherlock Holmes

Sherlock Holmes and other good detectives search for clues, examine all evidence, and deduce what actually happened. Similarly, successful investors, lenders, and analysts read financial reports and other information, searching for clues and deducing how the company actually performed in the past and how it is likely to perform in the future. This chapter describes the process of evaluating financial evidence.

Gathering Financial Data

The process of evaluating financial evidence begins with data collection. One should start by contacting the company of interest or

the SEC (at 450 5th Street, NW, Washington, DC 20549),* request-
ing the company's annual and quarterly financial statements and
other reports sent to the SEC: (1) Form 10-K, (2) annual reports,
(3) proxy statements, (4) Form 10-Q, (5) Form 8-K, (5) annual and
quarterly reports to shareholders, and (5) prospectuses (part of
securities registration statements). Additionally, to analyze public companies issuing new securities, one may obtain a prospectus from either the underwriter or the SEC. Alternatively, financial data can be obtained electronically (i.e., through Mead
Corporation's Lexis/Nexis database or Dow Jones's News Retrieval), through search services (i.e., Disclosure, Inc., or Federal
Filings, Inc.), or through secondary sources (i.e., Standard &
Poor's or Value Line).

A SUMMARY OF CORPORATE FILINGS

I. Regular Filings

  A. Annual

    Form 10-K[1]   All publicly held companies report
detailed financial results with the SEC
on an annual basis using Form 10-K.
This report, audited by an independent accountant, is due 90 days after
the close of the fiscal year.

    Annual report   Publicly held companies generally
report their financial results to shareholders once a year in an annual
report. This report, a condensed version of Form 10-K, contains the basic
financial statements, the accompanying footnotes, a report by an independent CPA, and a letter from the company president.

---

*The SEC also has nine regional offices located in Boston, New York,
Philadelphia, Atlanta, Chicago, Fort Worth, Denver, Los Angeles, and Seattle.

Proxy	A proxy statement is mailed to stockholders in connection with the annual stockholders' meeting. This document explains proposals to be voted on by shareholders, including such routine items as the reappointment of a company's accounting firm. More important, it contains information about management compensation, management stock options, special deals for management and directors, related-party transactions, and changes of auditors.

B. Quarterly

Form 10-Q	Publicly held companies must file quarterly reports within 45 days after the close of each quarter using Form 10-Q. This report, which is far less detailed than Form 10-K, is *not audited* by a CPA. It contains a balance sheet, a statement of operations and cash flow, footnotes, and management discussion and analysis (MD&A).

II. Irregular Filings

Form 8-K	Using Form 8-K, a company must inform the SEC of special events (within 15 days after their occurrence, except for auditor changes, which are due within 5 days), including changes in control of the company, acquisitions, dispositions, auditor changes, the resignation of directors, and bankruptcy.

(*Continued*)

II. Irregular Filings (*continued*)

Registration[2]   Whenever a publicly held company plans to issue securities, it must first file a registration statement, including a prospectus and exhibits, with the SEC (using Form S-1 or Form S-18 for initial public offerings). Along with the registration statement, it must submit a prospectus that describes the company's background, financial performance, and future plans. The prospectus is a detailed business plan which includes many valuable clues that can be used for predicting a company's future performance.

[1]Publicly held companies must file a Form 10-K, an annual shareholders' report, and a proxy. They have some flexibility concerning what to disclose in each one, so readers should view these three as an integrated document. A typical Form 10-K contains the following sections: Audited Balance Sheet (past two years), Audited Statement of Operations (past three years), Audited Cash Flow Statement (past three years), Footnotes to the Financial Statements Management Discussion and Analysis (MD&A), Auditor's Report, Liquidity Position and Capital Expenditures, Pending Litigation, Description of the Company's Business & History, Directors and Executive Officers, and Related-Party Transactions.

[2]Readers with an interest in investing in emerging growth companies (and specifically in discovering shenanigans hidden in such companies' prospectuses) will benefit from reading my previous book (written with Professor W. Keith Schilit of the University of South Florida), *Blue Chips and Hot Tips: Identifying Emerging Growth Companies Most Likely to Succeed* (New York Institute of Finance, 1992).

Searching for Shenanigans

With these documents in hand, the "shenanigan buster" is ready for action. So—where's a good place to start? Interestingly, not with the actual financial statements (i.e., the balance sheet, statement of operations*, and statement of cash flow). (Chapters 10 and 11 discuss how to find shenanigans on these financial statements.) Instead, the search should begin with the accompanying information, such as (1) the auditor's report, (2) proxy statements, (3) footnotes to financial statements, (4) the letter from the president, (5) management discussion and analysis (MD&A), and (6) Form 8-K.

USING THE DOCUMENTS TO FIND SHENANIGANS

Where to look	What to look for
Auditor's report (Part of Form 10-K)	Absence of opinion Qualified report Reputation of auditor
Proxy statement	Litigation Executive compensation Related-party transactions
Footnotes (Part of Form 10-K)	Accounting policies/changes Related-party transactions Contingencies or commitments
President's letter (Part of annual report)	Forthrightness
MD&A (Part of Form 10-K)	Specific concise disclosures Consistent with footnote disclosure
Form 8-K	Disagreements over accounting policies
Registration statement (for IPOs)	Past performance Quality of management and directors

---

*The terms "statement of income" and "statement of operations" are used synonymously in this book.

The Auditor's Report

Since the auditor has already spent weeks reviewing the financial records and searching for accounting tricks, first see what he or she has to say. Read the auditor's opinion first. Generally, this letter contains a "clean" opinion. However, if the auditor had a strong reservation about the company's financial condition or the fairness of its financial statements, he or she would generally "qualify" the report.

Watch for Qualified Opinions.   Investors should be cautious about investing in any company that receives a qualified opinion—even more so if it is a "going concern" qualification. That was just the opinion auditors Ernst & Young gave on Carolco Pictures' 1991 financial statements. Ernst indicated "substantial doubts" about the movie company's ability to continue as a going concern after posting a loss of $265 million. A "going concern" qualification warns investors and others that the company is experiencing major financial difficulties.

Be Wary When No Audit Committee Exists.   Another warning sign for investors is the absence of an audit committee composed of outside members of the board of directors. Such a committee serves as a buffer between management and the independent auditor. While companies listed on the New York Stock Exchange are required to have audit committees, the majority of publicly traded companies do not have such requirements. Investors should be concerned if (1) no audit committee exists, and/or (2) committee members appear not to be independent of management.

Proxy Statements

Although proxy statements are separate from the annual report, investors should consider them an integral part of the financial report. Astute investors read the proxy statement to search for important information that is not included in the financial reports, such as special compensation "perks" for officers and directors, as well as lawsuits and other contingent obligations facing the company. One such investor, Hugo Quackenbush, Senior Vice President of Charles Schwab & Co., describes proxy statements as follows:

> [T]hey are like a soap opera in black and white. Management has to disclose all the stuff they don't want to and investors can get more of the texture and flavor of a company reading the proxy statement than the glossy annual report.

Sometimes the news in a proxy statement is so significant that it causes the stock price to tumble. Consider the case of Lifetime Products, a company with one hot product: a patented, triple-edged auto windshield wiper. In early 1991 things looked great for the company's investors: The stock had soared from under $1 in 1990 to $14 in early 1991, and sales were expected to exceed $50 million in 1991, up from $3.3 million in 1989.

Lifetime Products dropped several bombshells, however, in its proxy statement. Specifically, one of the original investors sued Lifetime to force it to accelerate the payment of a $6 million debt. Additionally, two subsidiaries were paying big bonuses to the company's executives.

Although the litigation was settled out of court when management agreed to reduce its consulting compensation, investors apparently lost confidence in the company. Lifetime's market value, which in early 1991 exceeded $50 million, in mid-1992 was only $6 million.

More recently, the 1992 proxy statement for Kerr Glass Manufacturing provided some startling news about the compensation package of its chief executive officer (CEO). In addition to a $600,000 annual salary, he received extra compensation amounting to over $1 million: (1) forgiveness of a $528,319 loan given by the company in 1989 to help finance his primary residence, and (2) $354,567 to pay his taxes, related to the additional income resulting from the loan forgiveness.

Shareholders and officials of Institutional Shareholder Services, Inc., a shareholder rights organization, were furious about the size and the composition of the CEO's compensation. According to one activist: "This company isn't a bank. They shouldn't be in the business of making loans and forgiving loans."

Footnotes to Financial Statements

Appended to the financial statements are footnotes. They provide the reader with a wealth of information for assessing the financial condition of a company and the quality of its reported earnings. Specifically, the footnotes detail such matters as (1) accounting policies selected, (2) pending or imminent litigation, (3) long-term purchase commitments, (4) changes in accounting principles or estimates, (5) industry-specific notes (e.g., unbilled receivables for a government contractor), and (6) segment information showing healthy and unhealthy operations.

Many analysts agree that information in the footnotes is actually more important than what is shown on the financial statements. Kenneth Fisher, for example, wrote in *Forbes:*

> [T]he back of the report, the footnotes is where they hide the bad stuff they didn't want to disclose but had to...they bury the bodies where the fewest folks find them—in the fine print.

Favor Companies with Conservative Accounting Policies. Footnotes can indicate signs of "creative" accounting or gimmicks. Some footnotes should lead you to question not only the validity of the financial statements, but also the integrity of management. Companies that fail to use conservative accounting methods might demonstrate a lack of integrity in their financial reporting process. Indeed, many analysts place a premium on companies that use conservative accounting policies. In searching for excellent companies, for example, the widely respected analyst and shenanigan buster Thornton O'glove offers the following advice:

> Look for companies that use very conservative accounting principles. In my experience, if a company does not cut corners in its accounting, there's a good chance it doesn't cut corners in its operations. You know you've got your money with a high-quality management.

Be Alert for an Aggressive or Inappropriate Inventory Valuation. The selection of an inventory valuation method, which can substantially affect a company's reported profits, often

EVALUATING ACCOUNTING POLICIES

Accounting policy	Conservative	Aggressive
Revenue recognition	After sale, risks passed to buyer	At sale, although risk remains
Depreciation choice	Accelerated over shorter period	Straight line over longer period
Inventory method	LIFO (assuming prices are rising)	FIFO (assuming prices are rising)
Amortization of goodwill	Shorter period	Over 40 years
Estimate of warranty	High estimate	Low estimate
Estimate of bad debts	High estimate	Low estimate
Treatment of advertising	Expense	Capitalize
Loss contingencies	Accrue loss	Footnote only

indicates the degree of conservatism in a company's accounting policies. The most popular methods chosen are last-in, first-out (LIFO) and first-in, first-out (FIFO). LIFO charges the latest inventory costs as an expense first; conversely, FIFO charges the earliest costs first.

During inflationary periods (i.e., when inventory costs are rising), the differences between LIFO and FIFO could affect profits substantially. Under these circumstances LIFO generally produces lower reported profits for a company than does FIFO (resulting also in lower taxes and therefore in higher cash flows). FIFO under-values the rising costs of inventory and results in a higher level of reported profits. Thus FIFO is often considered a more "aggressive" inventory valuation technique. [Please note, however, that in the case of technology companies (for which component costs are often declining), LIFO is often more aggressive (since it undervalues costs, thereby overstating "true" earnings).]

Moreover, the choice of an inventory valuation method should be appropriate for the inventory being sold. Consider Home Shopping Network's (HSN) selection of the rarely used (but permissible under GAAP) specific identification method, rather than LIFO or FIFO, to value inventory. Specific identification, which enables a company to "manage" its profits, was especially questionable for HSN because that method should be used only for slow-moving, high-cost merchandise—hardly the type that HSN sold.

Company Profile

Home Shopping Network

Home Shopping Network used the specific identification method, enabling it to better "manage" its profits.

Home Shopping Network is a specialty retailer that markets a variety of consumer products by means of live, customer-interactive, sales programs televised over its own networks. The company evolved from management's experience using broadcast media to sell consumer goods in the Tampa Bay area of Florida. (From 1977 to 1982, a predecessor business sold consumer goods over the radio.) Although sales grew to over $1 billion in 1991, the stock disappointed investors. Valued at over $4 billion in 1987, the company was worth less than $500 million in mid-1992. See Fig. 2-1.

Consider Pending or Imminent Litigation. In addition to searching the footnotes for nonconservative accounting principles, note any pending or imminent litigation. (The litigation footnote is usually less informative than a company's response to item 3 on Form 10-K.) Such litigation may have serious consequences for a company's future operations. Consider Manville Corporation and its asbestos-related lawsuits. In 1982, the company filed for bankruptcy—a strategy undertaken not because of existing financial difficulties, but rather because of anticipated legal concerns about the settlement of numerous asbestos-related court cases that either had been or were expected to be filed against it.

Home Shopping Network Inc.

Stock Price Movement 1986–1990

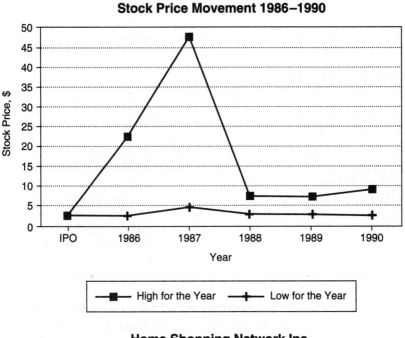

Home Shopping Network Inc.

Year	High	Low
	Price	
IPO	$ 3.00	$3.00
1986	$22.25	$3.00
1987	$47.00	$5.00
1988	$ 7.75	$3.38
1989	$ 7.63	$3.00
1990	$ 9.25	$2.88

Fig. 2-1.

Although it mentioned the lawsuits in the footnotes to its 1981 financial statements, Manville failed to include on the financial statements themselves an "estimated loss" and the related "reserve against future claims." In fact, Manville misled readers into concluding that its future obligation would be insignificant when its footnote stated:

> J-M believes that it has substantial defenses to these legal actions [referring to the asbestos lawsuits]. . . .

Unfortunately, as investors and others learned later, the subsequent litigation payments eventually forced Manville into bankruptcy.

Company Profile

Manville Corporation

Manville's financial report was misleading in that the company indicated the litigation would not likely have an adverse effect on its financial condition.

Manville is a leading producer of forest products and fiberglass. By 1982, it had settled over 4,100 asbestos cases and faced 17,000 more. The company was in Chapter 11 bankruptcy from 1982 through 1988, seeking protection from these claims. After working out a settlement with creditors, a smaller Manville Corporation emerged from bankruptcy in 1989. In mid-1992, its sales exceeded $2 billion, and its market value was approximately $385 million.

More recently, Exide Electronics indicated in a footnote to its December 1989 financial statements (prepared in connection with its initial public offering) that it had litigation pending in California. Investors who missed this note or failed to take the matter seriously were stung by the news in April 1990—just three months after the public offering—that the court had handed down a $14.9 million verdict against Exide. As a result, its stock price collapsed.

Question Long-Term Purchase Commitments. Besides noting litigation, footnotes also alert investors to long-term purchase commitments. Buried in the footnotes of Columbia Gas Systems' first-quarter 1991 10-Q was notification that the company had a long-term commitment to purchase natural gas at inflated prices. Investors who noted and understood the significance of this footnote should have been nervous. The company had signed a contract in early 1991 (during Operation Desert Storm in Kuwait), when gas prices were at their height. Since customers were not locked into buying this high-priced gas, investors should have concluded that Columbia would be unable to sell it at a profit. Sure enough, Columbia was unable to sell the gas, and in April 1991 it filed for bankruptcy. In subsequent lawsuits, investors and lenders alleged that Columbia misled them by failing to disclose a substantial contingent liability.

Company Profile

Columbia Gas Systems

Columbia Gas had signed a long-term commitment to purchase natural gas at inflated prices, leading to substantial losses when prices dropped in succeeding months.

Columbia Gas is a major supplier of natural gas and oil in the Middle Atlantic area. Its annual sales approach $1.4 billion, but have been declining in recent years. In mid-1991, Columbia Gas filed for bankruptcy, and its stock price fell more than 75 percent. Valued at more than $2 billion in early 1991, the company was worth $750 million in mid-1992. See Fig. 2-2.

Watch for Changes in Accounting Principles. As indicated earlier, management has substantial flexibility in choosing accounting principles, and that choice generally affects a company's profits. Investors and lenders should thus take note whenever a company changes accounting principles for no apparent reason. Such changes can also sometimes signal bookkeeping games to boost weak financial statements. Consider the following examples.

Union Carbide. During the first quarter of 1980, Union Carbide's earnings increased by $217 million. The increase resulted from three simple accounting changes: (1) changing from a conservative depreciation policy to a more liberal one, thus reducing the annual depreciation expense; (2) changing the procedure for handling investment credits arising out of the Internal Revenue Code; and (3) capitalizing interest costs incurred during construction instead of expensing them. Each of these changes boosted profits, and yet none was the result of an increase in businesses or other operating factors.

General Motors. Slowing down a company's depreciation schedule or changing its depreciation method can dress up earnings quite nicely. In 1988, according to stock analyst David Healy,

Columbia Gas Systems
Stock Price Movement 1991

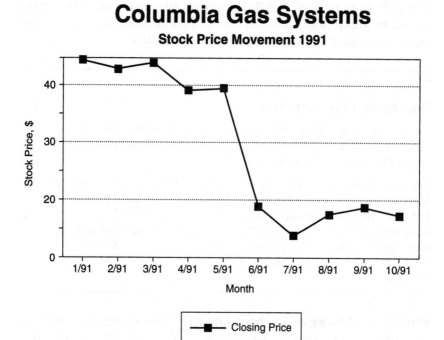

Closing Price

Columbia Gas Systems

Date	Price Close
1/91	$44.75
2/91	$43.13
3/91	$44.13
4/91	$39.38
5/91	$40.13
6/91	$19.13
7/91	$14.00
8/91	$18.00
9/91	$18.88
10/91	$17.88

Fig. 2-2.

GM was able to post record earnings directly because of its decision to liberalize its accounting policies. Healy calculated that about $1.8 billion of GM's $4.9 billion in profits came from such tricks: $790 million from changing its depreciation period for plant assets from 35 to 45 years, $480 million from changing its accounting for pensions, $217 million from changing its inventory valuation policies, and $270 million from changing its assumptions about the residual value of cars leased out by the company.

The Letter from the President

After reading the footnotes, you should turn to the front of the annual report, where you are greeted with a picture of and some words from the president. Sometimes, the president announces some recent event that will significantly hurt the company's future performance. But don't count on it. Unfortunately, the tone of this letter is almost invariably upbeat—regardless of real conditions. In a recent study intended to identify the words used most frequently to disguise a company in serious trouble, Professor Martin Kellman found that no word is more ominous than "challenging." His interpretation of "challenging": "[Y]our company has lost money, is losing money, and will continue to lose money." His recommendation: "[I]f the C-word appears in any form three or more times in the front pages of any annual report—sell immediately!"

Read the Letter from the President with a Grain of Salt. Many professional analysts agree that the letter from the president is used to bias the reader into thinking the company is doing better than it really is. Thornton O'glove describes the president's letter this way:

> It is designed to serve as a veil for the striptease—namely, to offer a hint of what is underneath, to indicate shape and form but not to permit too much insight.

O'glove also suggests reading the president's letter for the last three or four years to determine how previous predictions turned out. Like O'glove, Raymond DeVoe (an analyst with Legg Mason Wood Walker) has made a hobby of perusing annual reports and their letter from the president. DeVoe has developed a way of translating what the president is really saying. Here are a few of his "translations" of presidential declarations:

ANNUAL REPORT: "Your company is now poised for significant earnings growth."

(TRANSLATION: "We lost so much last year and wrote off everything possible, so earnings couldn't get much worse.")

ANNUAL REPORT: "These results were somewhat below the projections that management had announced publicly during the quarter."

(TRANSLATION: "We lied.")

ANNUAL REPORT: "The quarter's earnings contained a substantial contribution from a settlement arising from the involuntary termination of operating equipment."

(TRANSLATION: "If the plane hadn't crashed, we would have been in the red. Fortunately, only one was killed, and the insurance company paid off a helluva lot.")

While most letters from presidents are short on informative disclosure and long on fluff, Warren E. Buffett's (president of Berkshire Hathaway) letter stands out for its candor. Buffett often uses his letter to discuss mistakes that he has made and to reflect on important issues of the time. Of particular interest in his 1992 letter was Buffett's criticism of financial shenanigans used in the insurance industry to prop up earnings, stating:

> Loss-reserve data for the [insurance] industry indicate that there is reason to be skeptical of the outcome, and it may turn out that 1991's ratio should have been worse than was reported. In the long run, of course, trouble awaits managements that paper over operating problems with accounting maneuvers. Eventually, managements of this kind achieve the same result as the seriously-ill patient who tells his doctor: "I can't afford the operation, but would you accept a small payment to touch up the x-rays?

Focus on Management and Its Estimates. Reading the president's letter is a good way of assessing the integrity of management. Things to look for:

- Does management cast a rosy glow on unfavorable developments?

- Has there been a significant turnover of high-ranking managers from year to year? (That could be a tipoff of corporate turmoil.

For example, 4 of the 13 managers listed in the 1986 annual report of The Gap clothing chain's Banana Republic were absent from the 1987 report. This type of information is usually disclosed in the proxy statement.)

Management Discussion and Analysis (MD&A)

If the information in the president's letter lacks substance, try reading the section in the annual report and Form 10-K entitled "Management Discussion and Analysis" (MD&A). This section requires management to discuss specific issues on the financial statements and to assess its current financial situation, its liquidity, and its planned capital expenditures for the next year. It also is a good place to learn about management's candor. If the company is clearly having financial difficulties, the MD&A should level with the readers and not try to avoid or sugar-coat the problem. Thus, when Chrysler Corporation was running out of money in 1980 (shortly before the government bailed out the company), it should have leveled with and warned investors. Recently, the SEC has begun reading the MD&A section more critically. In 1992, the commission charged that the financial reports of Caterpillar, Inc. were misleading for failing to fully disclose problems at its Brazilian subsidiary.

Form 8-K

After reviewing the company's annual report (or Form 10-K), a good shenanigan buster should contact the SEC to learn whether there have been any recent Form 8-K filings for the company. Besides telling the investor about major acquisitions or divestitures by the company, Form 8-K highlights any changes in auditors. Such changes could offer clues to financial shenanigans, especially in those cases in which the auditors may have been fired because they found some problem they were unwilling to suppress.

A company that fires its auditor because of a disagreement over financial principles and then shops around for a new auditor more agreeable to its interpretation of GAAP has engaged in what is known as "opinion shopping." To prevent this practice, the SEC requires the company to file a Form 8-K, notifying the commission about the termination and any details about accounting disagreements. Unfortunately, few disagreements are ever actually disclosed in these filings.

A Look Ahead

Chapters 3 through 9 introduce seven major shenanigans, show how companies might use them to distort financial statements, and reveal how a shenanigan buster can catch them.

3

Shenanigan No. 1: Recording Revenue Too Soon

During the summer of 1991, I received a phone call from an excited young entrepreneur named Carol, who had a hot-selling computer software game. She wanted my assistance in finding capital for her growing business. When we met, she showed me her business plan, complete with glowing five-year projections. With my investigative mind set, I naturally asked her how and when she recognized revenue; Carol replied that revenue was recorded when the product was shipped out. I began questioning her about her accounting for refunds on sales, a significant factor since most software companies sell their products with a 30-day return policy (and returns can be considerable in that industry). I explained that, according to GAAP, not all of the cash received can be recorded as revenue at the time of shipment. Carol then argued that she needed to show a profit to obtain a bank line of credit and that if she did not include the entire amount received as revenue, her business would show a large loss. Sensing that I would not budge from my "interpretation" of GAAP, Carol decided to shop around for another accountant with a more "flexible" interpretation of the accounting rules.

Shenanigan No. 1: Recording Revenue Too Soon

Guiding principle: Revenue should be recorded after the earnings process has been completed and an exchange has occurred.

The most common shenanigan related to revenue recognition may be management recording it too early—either before the earnings process has been completed or before an exchange has occurred. The techniques generally used to "front-end load" revenue, as this process is known, are shipping goods before a sale is finalized, recording revenue after goods are shipped but while important uncertainties still remain, and recording revenue when services must still be performed in the future.

How It's Done

1. Shipping goods before a sale is finalized
2. Recording revenue when important uncertainties exist
3. Recording revenue when future services are still due

Technique No. 1: Shipping Goods Before a Sale Is Finalized

Generally Accepted Accounting Principles (GAAP) require that inventory be shipped out and exchanged for cash or another asset before revenue can be recorded. The specific accounting entry at the time the inventory is sold is shown in the following *Accounting Capsule.*

Accounting Capsule

Recording Sales on Account

Assume that a company sells merchandise costing $6,500 for $10,000.

Increase:	Accounts Receivable	10,000	
Increase:	Sales		10,000
Increase:	Cost of Goods Sold	6,500	
Decrease:	Inventory		6,500

As the capsule illustrates, a company should record sales revenue only after inventory has been shipped out and cash (or another asset) has been received in return. One shenanigan to watch for is the recording of revenue upon shipment of merchandise when no sale has yet occurred.

Watch for Early Shipping, Before the Sale Occurs.   The fiscal quarter is coming to a close and profits are sagging. What can a company do? Why not simply start shipping out merchandise and recording revenue, thereby boosting sales and profits? Merchandise is rushed out of the warehouse to customers toward the end of the year (even before the sales have taken place), and sales revenue is recorded. Since revenue is recognized under this method when an item is *shipped* to retailers or wholesalers, some manufacturers may be tempted to keep shipping their products during slow times—even if the retailers' shelves are overstocked. Automobile manufacturers have been doing this for years, thereby artificially increasing their sales.

Company Profile

Datapoint Corporation

Datapoint was charged by the SEC with recording revenue too early by, among other things, shipping goods before scheduled delivery dates.

Datapoint develops, manufactures, and markets local area network-based distributed and integrated information processing systems. During the early 1980s, the company was growing rapidly, with a market value exceeding $1.6 billion. However, the SEC launched an investigation into the company's accounting methods and charged that its 1981 profits had been overstated. The resulting disclosure contributed to the swift decline of the company's stock price in 1982. By 1989, its annual sales approached $270 million (but they have since declined slightly), and its market value in mid-1992 was approximately $35 million. See Fig. 3-1.

One company accused of such a shenanigan was computer maker Datapoint Corporation. The SEC charged that Datapoint used various tricks to boost its profits, including the recognition of sales revenue on (1) shipments of merchandise in advance of scheduled delivery dates, even in the absence of an express or implied agreement; (2) "partial" shipments of merchandise, containing only part of a customer's order; and (3) shipments of merchandise for which customers had canceled the orders (and had so informed Datapoint before shipment).

Long-Term Contracts Are the Exception.   It can be appropriate (and desirable) for a company to record revenue before it ships inventory. In particular, companies engaged in long-term construction contracts—in the aerospace and construction industries, for example—commonly accrue part of the revenue and profits during each year of construction.

Consider how aerospace giant Boeing might record revenue on a five-year contract to build commercial aircraft for American Airlines. It has two choices: wait until the end of the contract to record revenue and profits (the "completed-contract" approach), or record a part of revenue and profits during each year based on the amount completed [the "percentage-of-completion" method (also called the "percentage approach")].

The percentage approach is appropriate if the company seems likely to complete the contract, no important uncertainties exist, and accurate interim measures of the completion rate can be obtained. If important uncertainties exist, and/or reliable estimates cannot be obtained, however, the more conservative completed-contract approach should be used—with revenues and profits recorded at the end of the five years.

Nevertheless, Weigh Uncertainties for Companies Using the Percentage Method.   A decision to use the percentage method may be well intentioned but still have undesirable consequences. Consider how recent world events might cause the financial statements of certain defense companies using the percentage method to be misleading. In September 1991, President George Bush announced that the United States would begin eliminating nuclear armaments and scaling back the development of related weapon systems. As a result, the financial statements of many defense companies that use the percentage method overstated revenues (since revenue whose receipt was anticipated upon the completion of contracts could no longer be counted upon).

Datapoint Corporation
Stock Price Movement 1981–1990

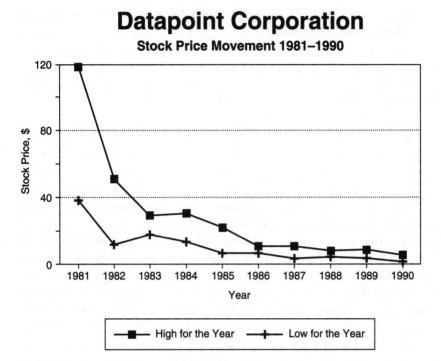

Datapoint Corporation

Year	Price High	Low
1981	$118.75	$38.75
1982	$ 51.88	$10.88
1983	$ 30.00	$17.75
1984	$ 30.50	$13.13
1985	$ 22.00	$ 4.50
1986	$ 9.25	$ 4.75
1987	$ 9.25	$ 3.38
1988	$ 5.75	$ 3.75
1989	$ 6.25	$ 3.00
1990	$ 4.38	$ 0.75

Fig. 3-1

Here's how the numbers might look for a company affected by President Bush's decision.

Contract price	$2.0 billion
Estimated costs	$1.5 billion
Estimated profit	$0.5 billion
Percent completed:	
Year 1	20%
Year 2	20%
Year 3	20%
Year 4	Canceled

Using the percentage approach, the company would have recorded 20 percent of the revenue (and profits) during years 1, 2, and 3. Thus the cumulative recorded revenue and profits would have been $1.2 billion and $300 million, respectively. Because of the President's decision to scale back nuclear weapons systems, however, this contract was canceled. As a result, the company would have erroneously recorded revenue and profit that it ultimately would not realize (and receive).

Look for Improper Use of the Percentage Method.   Aside from political uncertainties, several other practical problems must be considered before using the percentage approach. First, this method relies on estimates of future costs and future events; it can therefore be manipulated by distorting cost estimates or stage-of-completion records. Second, changes in estimates may be motivated more by a desire to control reported profits than by new information.

Partly because of the difficulty in verifying estimates, the percentage-of-completion method is susceptible to front-end loading of revenue and should not be used in such circumstances. This approach is particularly risky for new companies with uncertain products or markets. For example, Organogenesis—a young biotechnology company developing a new product for burn victims—was recording revenue of over $4 million for two long-term contracts. The company had yet to complete its work or receive the money.

But what would happen if the company fails to complete the project or fails to complete it within the required time or under

the agreed-upon conditions? As we saw with the defense contractor illustration, the reported revenue and profit would be
substantially overstated. For that reason, the percentage-of-completion method is considered an aggressive accounting practice
that can overstate earnings.

Company Profile

Organogenesis

Organogenesis is engaged in developing living organ
equivalents from human cells and tissue molecules. In part
because of the aggressive accounting methods used and in part
because of the company's failure to live up to investor
expectations, its stock price languished. Its annual sales totaled
$3.5 million in 1991, only slightly more than its annual net loss.
Valued at over $230 million in 1987, Organogenesis' market
value approximated $120 million in mid-1992. See Fig. 3-2.

Technique No. 2: Recording Revenue When Important Uncertainties Exist

A second technique for front-end loading of revenue is to record
it before important uncertainties have been resolved. Besides
shipping the goods to customers, GAAP requires that before revenue is recorded there must be a high probability that the goods
will not be returned and that the customer will pay for them. It
would be inappropriate to record revenue if:

- The risks and benefits of ownership have not been transferred
  to the buyer
- The buyer might return the goods
- The buyer might not pay for the goods

**Check Whether the Risks and Benefits Have Been
Transferred to the Buyer.**   When a company sells its accounts
receivable to a factor (similar to a bank), the sale could be "with
recourse" or "without recourse." If the transaction is without
recourse (i.e., risk is transferred to the factor), it is accounted for
as a sale. Conversely, if the transaction is with recourse (i.e., risk

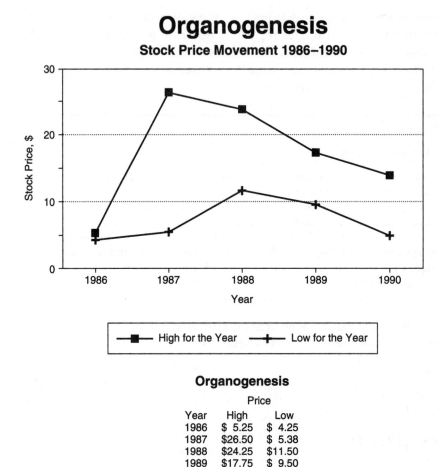

Organogenesis
Stock Price Movement 1986–1990

Organogenesis

Year	Price High	Low
1986	$ 5.25	$ 4.25
1987	$26.50	$ 5.38
1988	$24.25	$11.50
1989	$17.75	$ 9.50
1990	$13.88	$ 4.63

Fig. 3-2.

is still with the seller), it cannot be recorded as a sale. Sales revenue is recorded only *after* the risk has been transferred.

An example of a company recording revenue before risk was transferred is Financial Corporation of America (FCA). The SEC charged FCA with prematurely recognizing revenue from certain "buy/sell" transactions during the period June 30, 1980, through December 31, 1982. These transactions permitted FCA to recognize gains on "sales" of land and on interest and loan fees in connection with the transactions.

Company Profile

Financial Corporation of America

Financial Corporation of America (FCA) was charged with recognizing revenue before it was earned.

FCA was a Standard & Poor's 500 stock (with $34 billion in assets on the day it was rescued) and one of the 10 largest S&L holding companies in the United States. It was the holding company for scandal-plagued American Savings and Loan Association. Like many other S&Ls that dabbled in risky real estate and junk bonds during the 1980s, the company was bankrupt by 1992. See Fig. 3-3.

Determine Whether the Buyer Is Likely to Return the Goods. Many businesses permit the buyer a "right of return" if it is not satisfied with the goods. That provision is true, for example, for companies that sell consumer goods (such as appliances and automobiles) and for publishers that sell books to bookstores on a "right-of-return" basis (the books can be returned if they are unsold). Thus, although a publisher has made a sale to the bookstore and there has been an arm's-length exchange, it would be inappropriate to record all the revenue (since some books will surely be returned).

Consider Whether the Buyer Is Likely to Pay. A sale might be contingent on either the customer's receipt of funding from third-party sources or the customer's subsequent resale to a third party; in either case, no revenue should be recorded at the time of sale. The following sections give examples of companies that recorded revenue even when important contingencies existed that should have raised doubt about whether the buyer would pay.

Check Whether the Buyer Has Financing to Pay. When a sale depends on the buyer receiving financing, revenue should not be recorded until the financing is in place. This is common in real estate transactions, in which the sale depends on the buyer's ability to obtain a mortgage.

One company that failed to wait for financing commitments was Stirling Homex Corporation, a manufacturer of completely installed modular dwelling units. Stirling sold homes to low-

FCA Corporation

Stock Price Movement 1981–1987

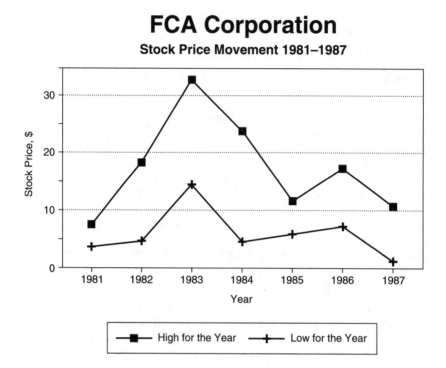

Year	Price High	Low
1981	$ 7.38	$ 3.75
1982	$18.50	$ 4.63
1983	$32.75	$14.38
1984	$24.38	$ 4.00
1985	$11.25	$ 5.25
1986	$17.25	$ 6.88
1987	$10.38	$ 1.00

FCA Corporation

Fig. 3-3.

income buyers who had limited resources, most of whom
obtained financing through the U.S. Department of Housing and
Urban Development (HUD). Stirling improperly recorded revenue when HUD signed a preliminary commitment of funding,
rather than waiting for the final approval. As a result, Stirling
recorded revenue for certain customers who ultimately failed to
receive financing; and the financial statements that portrayed
Stirling as a healthy, prosperous company with increasing sales

and earnings, in reality, covered up the company's serious business and financial problems.

Company Profile

Stirling Homex

Stirling Homex improperly recorded revenue before the buyer had obtained financing.

Home-builder Stirling Homex went public in February 1970 at $16.50 per share. In July 1972, Stirling filed for bankruptcy. Subsequent to this filing, the SEC began an investigation of Stirling's financial reporting for the period 1970 to 1972. It concluded that the reports were false and misleading.

Company Profile

Storage Technology Corporation

Storage Technology was charged with recognizing revenue too soon, since important contingencies existed and buyers were not yet obligated to pay.

Storage Technology designs, manufactures, and markets information storage retrieval products for the high-performance end of the computer industry. The company was flying high during the early 1980s, with a market value exceeding $1.5 billion in 1981. However, the SEC charged that the company's 1982–1985 financial statements were false and misleading, and in October 1984, the company filed for bankruptcy. Several years later it emerged from bankruptcy, freed of all its debt, and its stock price subsequently catapulted back to over $1.5 billion. See Fig. 3-4.

Determine Whether the Customer Is Obligated to Pay. If the buyer is not obligated to pay until a later event, revenue should not be recorded until that event occurs. One company that violated this rule was Storage Technology Corporation. The SEC charged that, during 1982, the company started recording revenue upon shipment to customers, even though the customers were not obligated to pay until after the equipment had been installed. Moreover, the industry practice was to allow customers to cancel legally binding orders any time before acceptance of the equipment. Such acceptance never occurred before the equipment was installed. Major uncertainties existed concerning the customers' willingness to complete the transactions, in part because the marketplace was unsure whether a new state-of-the-art disk drive would be available from a competitor.

Technique No. 3: Recording Revenue When Future Services Are Still Due

A third method of recording revenue too soon is to record it when received, even though some future services must still be performed. Consider the receipt by McDonald's of an initial payment from a franchisee. Because a part of that payment is unearned at the time of receipt (since future services must still be performed), McDonald's should record that portion as a liability and the rest as revenue. According to GAAP, when cash is received but services or some other obligation remains, the following accounting entry should be made.

Accounting Capsule

Recording Revenue Received in Advance

Assume that a company receives a $10,000 advance for future services.

Increase:	Cash	10,000	
Increase:	Unearned Revenue (a liability)		10,000

When the services are later performed, the revenue will be recorded as follows:

Decrease:	Unearned Revenue	6,000	
Increase:	Revenue Earned		6,000

A part or all of the revenue will be deferred until the later period when it is earned.

Storage Technology Corp.
Stock Price Movement 1980–1990

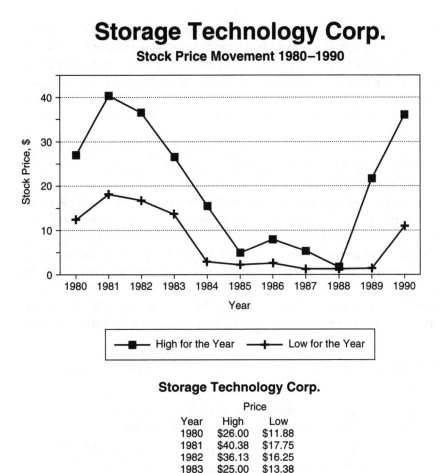

Storage Technology Corp.

		Price
Year	High	Low
1980	$26.00	$11.88
1981	$40.38	$17.75
1982	$36.13	$16.25
1983	$25.00	$13.38
1984	$14.63	$ 2.00
1985	$ 3.88	$ 1.50
1986	$ 7.63	$ 1.75
1987	$ 5.00	$ 1.13
1988	$ 2.00	$ 1.25
1989	$21.25	$ 1.63
1990	$35.25	$11.00

Fig. 3-4.

Watch for Hasty Recognition of Franchise Revenue.

Recording revenue when future services are due is not uncommon in accounting for franchisers who receive a substantial upfront payment that will be earned over several years. One troublesome accounting issue affecting franchisers involves revenue recognition from the sale of "area development rights." These are contracts sold by the company granting a developer the exclusive right to open franchises in a particular territory. In return, the developer traditionally pays the company a nonrefundable, up-front fee.

For years, franchisers have been recording these up-front fees as current income—that is, none of it was recorded as "unearned revenue." But the SEC argued that until the franchise units are open and operating, franchisers have yet to earn the total revenue; thus a portion should be deferred. Clearly, this practice of front-end loading of revenues results in artificially higher reported profits than is considered appropriate.

As one example, Jiffy Lube (the Baltimore-based franchiser of quick oil change centers) was charged in a civil lawsuit with front-end loading franchise revenue and overstating its 1988 profits. The company was forced to restate its financial statements, causing its profits to fall by 75 percent. In 1989, it recorded a loss of $79 million, compared to a profit of $7 million in 1988.

Company Profile

Jiffy Lube International

Jiffy Lube was charged by the SEC with recognizing up-front fees as revenue, even though future services were required.

Jiffy Lube franchises and operates 1,107 automobile oil change, fluid maintenance, and lubrication centers. The company was growing rapidly in 1986–1987, as was its stock price. As losses began rising and investor excitement declined in 1988, however, the stock price plummeted. In 1991, the company was acquired by Pennzoil Company. See Fig. 3-5.

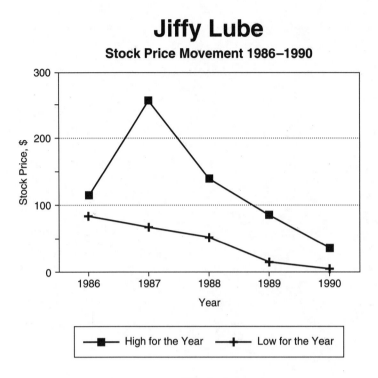

Jiffy Lube

Stock Price Movement 1986–1990

Jiffy Lube

Year	Price High	Low
1986	$115.00	$78.75
1987	$252.50	$65.00
1988	$138.75	$48.75
1989	$ 85.00	$13.75
1990	$ 30.00	$ 3.50

Fig. 3-5.

4

Shenanigan No. 2: Recording Bogus Revenues

Before relying on representations in financial reports, successful investors first ascertain whether those reports tell the economic story of a company fairly and completely. In one sense investors are like art dealers, trying to separate the real thing from fakes. Without sufficient training and a keen eye, identifying a fake may be difficult, as the following story by Arthur Koestler in *The Act of Creation* illustrates.

After purchasing a canvas signed "Picasso," an art dealer traveled all the way to Cannes, where Picasso was working in his studio, to discover whether it was genuine. Picasso cast a single look at the canvas and announced, "It's a fake."

A few months later the dealer bought another canvas signed "Picasso." Again he traveled to Cannes; and again Picasso, after a single glance, grunted: "It's a fake."

"But cher maître," expostulated the dealer, "it so happens that I saw you with my own eyes working on this very picture several years ago."

Picasso shrugged: "I often paint fakes."

One example of a "fake" on financial statements is fictitious revenue. This chapter describes tricks that companies may use to record such fictitious, or "bogus," revenue and how a shenanigan buster can uncover them.

Shenanigan No. 2: Recording Bogus Revenues

Guiding principle: Revenue should be recorded after the earnings process has been completed and an exchange has occurred.

A second shenanigan related to revenue recognition occurs when a company receives cash or other assets in nonsales transactions but still records sales revenue. Techniques used to record bogus revenue are classifying as income gains from exchanging similar assets, improperly classifying credits received from suppliers as revenue, and creating "income" by using bogus estimates on interim financial statements.

How It's Done

1. Recording income on the exchange of similar assets
2. Recording refunds from suppliers as revenue
3. Using bogus estimates on interim financial reports

Technique No. 1: Recording Income on the Exchange of Similar Assets

According to federal income tax law, no gain is recorded when a company exchanges similar property with another company. Because of this tax incentive, such exchanges are common in the real estate industry. This technique was commonly used by S&Ls to boost their reported profits.

Be Alert for Revenue Recorded on the Exchange of Property. Similar to the tax rules, GAAP permits no gain to be recorded on an exchange of similar property. Instead, the newly acquired assets should be recorded at the book value (not fair market value) of the asset given up.

Accounting Capsule

Recording Exchange of Similar Assets

Assume that a company exchanges property having a book value of $2,500 (but a market value of $10,000) for a *similar* piece of property.

Correct entry:			
New Asset	2,500		(book value)
Old Asset		2,500	(book value)
Incorrect entry:			
New Asset	10,000		(market value)
Old Asset		2,500	(book value)
Gain		7,500	

Two examples of companies that tried to boost weak profits by including "gains from sale of real estate" when all they did was exchange it for similar assets are Penn Central and MDC Holdings.

Penn Central. In a 1968 transaction, Penn Central claimed to have "gained" $21 million by exchanging its interest in the old Madison Square Garden Center and in the Penn Plaza office building for a 25 percent interest in the new Madison Square Garden. Although it received no cash, Penn Central recorded a gain by valuing the new Garden stock at $25.7 million and subtracting the $4.6 million carrying value of assets.

Based on GAAP, no gain should have been recorded (since Penn Central simply exchanged one piece of property for another, neither receiving nor paying cash). The SEC agreed, charging that Penn Central violated GAAP by "[substituting] an investment in one form for essentially the same investment in another form." There was no change in economic interests in Madison Square Garden, the principal asset involved; and Penn Central's intent was clearly not to dispose of its economic interest in the facilities exchanged.

MDC Holdings. Nearly 20 years after investors were tricked by Penn Central, home builder and real estate developer MDC Holdings reminded us how history repeats itself. On August 31, 1987, MDC sold one commercial and two residential tracts in a Riverside County, California, development known as Ranchos

Acacias for $14.9 million. MDC received cash for the property, recognizing a gain of $2.178 million on the sale, and deferred an additional $858,000 of the gain in connection with project development work that it was obligated to perform. On the very same day as the Ranchos Acacias sale, MDC purchased approximately 963 acres of residential property in a development near Phoenix known as Estrella, paying $16.862 million ($4.216 million in cash and $12.646 million in a promissory note).

According to GAAP, whenever a company exchanges similar assets (such as one piece of real estate for another), no gain or loss should be recorded. Instead, the new asset should be recorded at the book value of the asset sold. In effect, since the seller is in a similar position both before and after the sale, no revenue or gain should be recognized.

Clearly, MDC should have accounted for these transactions as an exchange of similar properties. Instead, it recorded the sale of the three Ranchos Acacias tracts and its purchase of the Estrella property as separate transactions.

Company Profile

MDC Holdings

MDC Holdings was charged by the SEC with improperly recording revenue and gains from selling assets, when in substance the risks and benefits of ownership had not yet transferred to the buyer.

MDC constructs, sells, and finances residential housing and acquires and develops land for its own building activity. During 1986–1987, as real estate values were climbing, so too were MDC's sales and profits. However, the company was stung by both an SEC enforcement action (charging that the 1987 financial statements were false and misleading) and a softening real estate market, leading to the company's decline. See Fig. 4-1.

Technique No. 2: Recording Refunds from Suppliers as Revenue

Companies receive cash for a variety of reasons, only some of which relate to revenue earned. One example is the receipt of refunds from suppliers or other vendors for returned merchandise.

MDC Holdings
Stock Price Movement 1984–1991

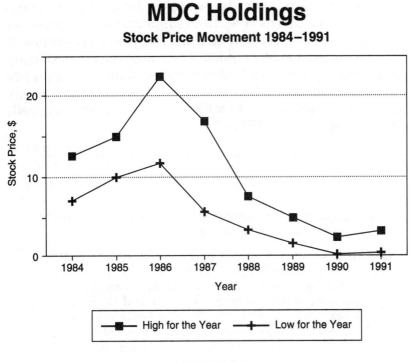

MDC Holdings

	Price	
Year	High	Low
1984	$12.75	$ 7.38
1985	$14.63	$10.00
1986	$22.50	$11.38
1987	$16.25	$ 5.25
1988	$ 6.88	$ 2.63
1989	$ 3.75	$ 1.00
1990	$ 1.50	$ 0.09
1991	$ 2.25	$ 0.28

Fig. 4-1.

Question How Retailers Account for Returned Goods.
Retailers periodically receive cash refunds (or credits) from suppliers and other vendors for inventory purchases that the retailer has returned. The proper accounting treatment for such refunds is to record a purchase return—not sales revenue.

Sometimes retailers overstate their sales, though, by recordings as revenues the credits received from suppliers for misshipments. For example, the SEC recently charged that L.A. Gear improperly classified as income $4.7 million in one-time vendor credits (for supplier misshipments and other sourcing troubles) that it had not actually collected. After restating its financial reports, L.A. Gear reported a net loss of $4 million, down from the originally reported net income of $258,000.

Company Profile

L.A. Gear

L.A. Gear was charged by the SEC with overstating its income by including credits from vendors as revenue.

L.A. Gear designs, manufactures, and markets athletic leisure footwear, sportswear, and casual apparel. In 1992 it posted a six-month loss of $12 million on declining sales of $350 million. With intense competition from Nike and Reebok, its profits and stock price slumped badly after having been a strong performer for many years. Though it was valued at $1.6 billion in 1990, by mid-1992 the company was worth only $250 million. See Fig. 4-2.

Technique No. 3: Using Bogus Estimates on Interim Financial Reports

The preparation of annual financial statements requires management to estimate a variety of issues, including sales returns, future warranty costs, and the longevity of plant and equipment. The preparation of quarterly financial statements requires management to make additional (and often more difficult) estimates.

Determine Whether the Estimates Are Realistic.   One of the most significant quarterly estimates involves the ending inventory and the related cost of goods sold. (For annual financial statements, inventory is counted physically; for quarterly reports, however, counting would be impractical.)

A common method of computing inventory and cost of sales is based on a company's estimate of its gross profit rate (gross profit

LA Gear Inc.

Stock Price Movement 1986–1991

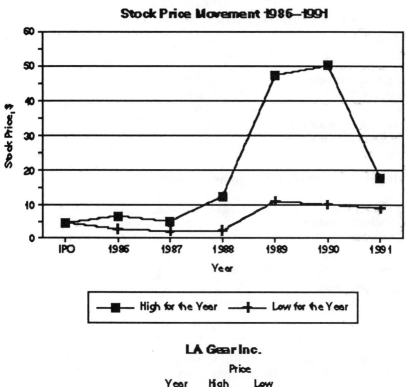

Year	High	Low
IPO	$ 2.88	$ 2.88
1986	$ 6.20	$ 2.00
1987	$ 3.50	$ 1.50
1988	$11.90	$ 2.30
1989	$45.80	$10.80
1990	$50.38	$ 9.75
1991	$17.63	$ 9.00

LA Gear Inc.

Price

Fig. 4-2.

divided by sales). This method (known as the "gross margin" or "gross profit" method) is perfectly legitimate. But because a fictitious estimate would distort the gross profit for the period, it should be used with great care. Indeed, the use of an inflated gross profit percentage would reduce the cost of goods sold and thereby overstate net income.

Accounting Capsule

Gross Margin (Profit) Method

Assume:

Beginning inventory	$125,000
Net purchases	450,000
Sales	600,000
Estimated gross profit	32%
Estimated cost of goods	68%

Ending inventory is estimated as follows:

Beginning inventory	$125,000
Net purchases	450,000
Cost of goods available	$575,000
Cost of goods sold ($600,000 × 68%)	408,000
Ending inventory	$167,000

Kaypro Computer Company. The SEC sued Kaypro Computer in November 1987, alleging that its Form 10-Q for the second and third quarters of fiscal year 1984 was false and misleading because the company had used an incorrect percentage in applying the gross profit method. The company used a cost of sales percentage of 57 to compute inventory during those periods—far below the 74 percent figure that a year-end audit determined it should have used.

Company Profile

Kaypro Computer Company

Kaypro Computer Company was charged by the SEC with overstating its quarterly profits by using an improper estimate that overstated its ending inventory and its profits.

Kaypro develops, manufactures, and markets portable computers for business and personal users. From its incorporation in 1953 until it began developing microcomputers in 1981, Kaypro was engaged exclusively in developing, manufacturing, and selling sophisticated electronic instruments used primarily in aerospace, defense, and industrial applications. When it went public in 1983, Kaypro had annual sales in excess of $80 million and was valued at approximately $360 million. An SEC investigation, however, found that its 1984 financial statements were misleading, and the company's fortunes rapidly deteriorated. Shortly thereafter, Kaypro filed for bankruptcy. See Fig. 4-3.

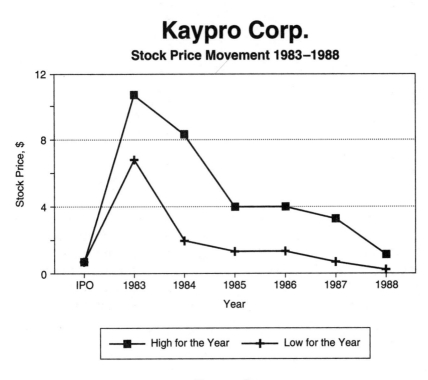

Kaypro Corp.
Stock Price Movement 1983–1988

Kaypro Corp.

Year	Price High	Low
IPO	$ 0.59	$0.59
1983	$10.63	$6.63
1984	$ 8.25	$2.00
1985	$ 4.00	$1.25
1986	$ 4.00	$1.25
1987	$ 3.25	$0.63
1988	$ 0.88	$0.25

Fig. 4-3.

5

Shenanigan No. 3: Boosting Income with One-Time Gains

When a magician wants to make a rabbit appear out of thin air, he may use a special potion, tap with a wand, or say the magical word "abracadabra." Not to be outdone, managers have their own version of creating something from nothing when it comes to profits. Managers don't need special props, though, and they don't need to use special words like abracadabra. All they need to know are a few easy-to-use techniques.

Boosting profits with accounting tricks and one-time gains may make managers happy; but investors and lenders who rely on such misleading financial reports aren't always so thrilled. Such reports often present an image of a healthy company when in reality the opposite is true. For example, consider how investors in and lenders to The Charter Company must have felt when, shortly after reporting a $50.4 million profit in 1983, the company filed for bankruptcy. Were there no warning signs in the financial statements that the reported profits were misleading?

To answer that question, we would have to take a closer look at the company's 1983 statement of income. In doing so, we would find that while the bottom line was favorable, most of the company's income derived from nonoperating activities. If an analyst had adjusted net income to exclude all nonrecurring or nonoperating items, the company would have looked quite sick. In fact, as shown below, Charter lost over $64 million from its normal recurring operating activities.

1983 reported *income* from continuing operations	$ 50,382
Subtract:	
Change in estimate of asset	3,003
Liquidation of LIFO layers	12,803
Gain from contract renegotiation	33,600
Gain on exchange of investment	17,125
Equity in earnings in excess of dividends	117,958
Add:	
Write-down of refinery	49,428
Write-down of tanker	7,772
Equity in net losses in affiliates	12,511
Adjusted *loss* from recurring operations	$(64,396)

As The Charter Company's unhappy investors and lenders learned, one must be alert for one-time techniques used by management to boost weak profits. This chapter describes various accounting gimmicks involving nonoperating and nonrecurring income that inflate (or distort) profits. These shenanigans represent comparatively minor deceptions, but they are still disconcerting.

Shenanigan No. 3: Boosting Income with One-Time Gains

Guiding principle: Revenue should be recorded after the earnings process has been completed and an exchange has occurred. Similarly, gains should be reported only after an exchange has taken place.

How It's Done

1. Boosting profits by selling undervalued assets
2. Boosting profits by retiring debt

3. Failing to segregate unusual and nonrecurring gains or losses from recurring income
4. Burying losses under noncontinuing operations

Technique No. 1: Boosting Profits by Selling Undervalued Assets

One technique that may be used to increase a company's income is to sell appreciated assets at prices above their cost (or book value). If such assets were recorded at unrealistically low book values, the resulting gain from their sale would be substantial. Consequently, investors and lenders should look critically at nonrecurring gains resulting from selling undervalued assets—especially if the sale makes no apparent economic sense.

Undervalued assets on the balance sheet are most common in the following situations:

- A company acquired assets in a business combination that was accounted for as a pooling of interest.
- A company uses the LIFO inventory method (especially with many inventory pools).
- A company acquired real estate (or other investments) years ago that has appreciated considerably in value.

Watch for the Sale of Pooled Assets Acquired in a Business Combination.   When a company is acquired in a "pooling-of-interest" (or "pooling") transaction, its assets are recorded on the combined company's balance sheet at their book value at the time of the combination. (The pooling method generally applies when no cash is paid—that is, there is simply an exchange of stock.)

If the acquired company's assets had been purchased years earlier, their book value may be substantially less than their current market value. That sets the stage for an accounting trick: selling off those assets at their fair market value and recording an instant gain. By selling such assets—which have not increased in value since the acquisition—a company releases "suppressed profits" created as a result of its initially recording the assets for far less than their fair market value.

The Meaning and Significance of Suppressed Profits

Gains are reported whenever a company sells assets at prices exceeding their original cost. It is natural that as assets are held over several years their value would increase, and gains would be reported when they are sold. If, however, recently purchased assets are recorded at less than their true fair market value (as in the case of assets acquired through a pooling of interest), a company would report a "windfall" gain when those assets are sold. Thus the sale of assets recorded at artificially low amounts enables a company to record a gain by releasing suppressed profits.

Sale of Assets Acquired in a Pooling Transaction

In an example of a business combination accounted for under the pooling method, a company acquires a subsidiary by exchanging stock with a market value of $1 million (but a book value of $200,000). The company holds the subsidiary for one year before selling it for $1.1 million. Clearly, the company's economic gain is $100,000. Because of a quirk in GAAP, however, the company would report a gain of $900,000—which includes the suppressed profit received by recording the asset initially for less than its fair market value of $1 million.

The pooling method is perfectly acceptable under GAAP. However, investors and lenders should discount profits and gains that resulted from selling assets that had been recorded at less than fair market value (and which, consequently, had an inherent "suppressed profit" at the time they were acquired).

General Electric.   General Electric (GE) was able to use the pooling method to help boost its profits when it acquired Utah International in 1976 by exchanging stock worth approximately $1.9 billion. GE recorded Utah's assets at their book value of $547.8 million, thus suppressing about $1.4 billion in value. The unrecorded asset value would be reflected as a gain as soon as GE sold those assets. Moreover, even if the assets were not later sold, their below-market valuation allowed GE to understate its expenses (cost of sales and depreciation) and thereby overstate net income.

Look Closely at Inventory Recorded under the LIFO Method. Similar to (but much more common than) the sale of assets acquired in a pooling transaction is the selling by a LIFO (last-in, first-out) company of inventory recorded on the books at below-market prices. Under LIFO, one of the more popular inventory valuation methods, the latest costs (generally the highest ones) are charged first against sales. The effects of charging higher costs against initial sales are twofold: Profits in the current year are lower, but those in later years (when lower-cost inventory is charged as it is being liquidated) will be higher. Here's how it works.

Accounting Capsule

Inventory Valuation Techniques

Assume that you purchased inventory three times this year:

10 units @ $200
15 units @ $220
18 units @ $225

Then you sold 30 units for $400 apiece during the year.

According to LIFO, you would assign the latest costs against sales as cost of goods sold. The cost of goods sold would be $6,690 (18 units @ $225 + 12 units @ $220). Your profit using LIFO would be $5,310 ($12,000 − $6,690). The remaining 13 units would remain in inventory and would be charged as cost of goods sold when they are sold in a future period.

A trick that LIFO companies might use to boost profits in future years is the quick liquidation (i.e., within a single reporting period) of a substantial portion of inventory that is listed on the balance sheet at very low prices. Using the illustration above, note that when the company sells its remaining 13 units of inventory, the cost of goods sold will be recorded at $200 for some units and $220 for others—that is, at a lower level than the current costs. Thus, whenever a company has a substantial liquidation of inventory within a single reporting period, unrealistically low prior-period costs will be charged against sales—providing a one-time boost to profits.

Be Alert for Tricks with LIFO Pools. A refinement of the LIFO method is to subdivide inventory into small groupings (or "inventory pools") representing each product sold. Such pools allow management to be more precise in selecting a cost to charge

---

Accounting Capsule

Using LIFO Pools

A company initially groups all its inventory together: 10 units @ $200; 15 units @ $220; and 18 units @ $225. Then it sells 30 units for $400 apiece during the year. Since all the units are grouped together, under LIFO it would charge $6,690 (18 units @ $225 and 12 units @ $220) as expense.

Now, assume instead that the company arbitrarily establishes the following three LIFO pools:

Pool A	Pool B	Pool C
1 unit @ $200	1 unit @ $200	8 units @ $200
2 units @ $220	2 units @ $220	11 units @ $220
6 units @ $225	1 unit @ $225	11 units @ $225

By selecting all units from Pool C (to take one example of the company's pool selection possibilities), its cost of goods sold would be $6,495 (8 units @ $200, 11 units @ $220, and 11 units @ $225). The reader should note that cost of goods sold is lower not only because of the particular pool chosen (which in this case was a relatively low-cost pool), but more generally because the policy allows a company to include some of the "first-in" costs from one pool before it considers the "last-in" costs from another (although the selection of units primarily from pools top-heavy with lower-cost inventory does indeed accentuate the effect and result in an even greater differential for the cost of goods sold).

---

as cost of goods sold. However, it also provides management with greater leeway in assigning a level of cost of goods sold to expense for that period. Indeed, the greater the number of inventory pools, the greater is the flexibility to manipulate profits. Consider the illustration in the preceding accounting capsule.

One company that used inventory pools to boost profits improperly was Stauffer Chemical Company. According to an SEC complaint, Stauffer overstated earnings by 25 percent by creating numerous meaningless inventory pools. Specifically, the SEC objected to Stauffer's decision to increase the number of its pools from 8 to 288. By selling off its LIFO inventory from "select" low-cost inventory pools, Stauffer created sudden surges of earnings.

Especially after years of high inflation and a buildup of inventory, the "real" inventory value under LIFO will be suppressed (since inventory includes the cost of purchases that may have taken place years ago). When a company begins liquidating its inventory, the result is an instant jump in profits—which is certain to delight its managers.

Company Profile

Stauffer Chemical Company

Stauffer Chemical was charged by the SEC with overstating its profits by creating meaningless inventory pools.

Stauffer manufactured and sold chemicals and chemical-related products until the mid-1980s. Its fortunes declined rapidly after the government filed suit in 1984, alleging false and misleading financial statements. Although its stock price rose slightly the following year, it filed for bankruptcy. See Fig. 5-1.

Watch for Gains from the Sale of Undervalued Investments, Including Real Estate. Inventory is only one example of assets that might be recorded on the books at prices far below current market value. Other assets, such as real estate and other investments, may have been acquired years ago at much lower prices and will provide a company with instant profits when they are sold.

Stauffer Chemical Company
Stock Price Movement 1978–1985

Stauffer Chemical Company

Year	Price High	Low
1978	$49.25	$34.00
1979	$44.50	$17.75
1980	$24.38	$14.50
1981	$27.33	$18.75
1982	$28.38	$17.00
1983	$31.75	$22.13
1984	$25.75	$15.75
1985	$28.13	$17.25

Fig. 5-1.

Assume, for instance, that a developer acquires land for $200,000 and that the land appreciates over time to a value of $2 million. The land is then transferred to a corporation for development. Since the owners are the same, the land will be recorded at its original cost of $200,000. If the land is then sold, the $1.8 million in suppressed value will gradually be reflected as earnings of the new entity, creating the impression of a successful operation.

Assets other than real estate may also be recorded on the books at amounts far below their current value. By selling off such assets (and releasing suppressed values), companies may be able to record large one-time gains—doing wonders to what may otherwise be a weak financial reporting position. Consider how TIE/Communications' anemic 1983 profits got a shot in the arm by the sale of some investments at a substantial gain, so that the company was able to post a profit of almost $10 million (which represented almost one-third of the total net income for the year).

Although a company that reports large gains from selling assets that have appreciated in value is not violating GAAP, it can mislead readers by painting a favorable picture that hides losses from recurring operating activities.

Company Profile

TIE/Communications

TIE/Communications' 1983 profits were artificially high because it included one-time gains from sale of assets.

TIE/Communications designs, manufactures, and sells telecommunication products, including digitally controlled telephone systems, peripheral data products, and high-traffic phone systems. During the 1980s it was growing rapidly, a fact that was reflected in a market value approaching $1.4 billion. Its business began to weaken, however, and in 1991 TIE posted a net loss totaling $33 million. By mid-1992, TIE's market value approached $240 million. See Fig. 5-2.

It is important to note that recording gains from the sale of assets that have appreciated in value is perfectly acceptable under GAAP. Nonetheless, investors should be especially critical of companies with weak operating profits that continually try to prop up net income by selling undervalued assets, particularly when the sale comes at the end of a quarter or a year.

Technique No. 2: Boosting Profits by Retiring Debt

A second technique for artificially boosting profits with a one-time gain (and which is permissible under GAAP) is to retire debt

TIE Communications

Stock Price Movement 1979–1990

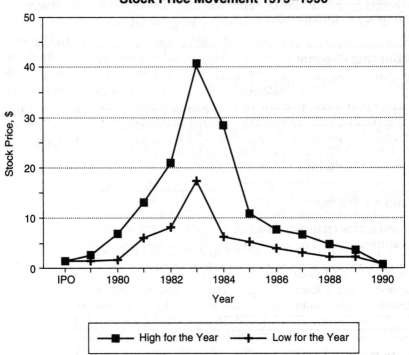

 — High for the Year   —+— Low for the Year

TIE Communications

Year	Price High	Low
IPO	$ 0.92	$ 0.92
1979	$ 1.62	$ 0.87
1980	$ 5.88	$ 1.13
1981	$11.88	$ 4.38
1982	$20.88	$ 6.63
1983	$40.38	$17.00
1984	$28.38	$ 5.50
1985	$10.63	$ 4.13
1986	$ 7.13	$ 2.75
1987	$ 5.88	$ 1.75
1988	$ 3.75	$ 1.13
1989	$ 2.50	$ 1.13
1990	$ 0.31	$ 0.31

Fig. 5-2.

early, particularly when it makes no apparent sense to do so. Shenanigan busters should be especially concerned when a company retires inexpensive debt only to replace it shortly thereafter with more expensive debt.

Accounting Capsule

Recording Retirement of Debt

Assume that a company with a long-term note payable of $1,000 (with a current market value of $750), paying 10 percent, decides to retire this debt and issue new debt at 11 percent. In substance, the company is replacing a $1,000 note (face amount) with a similar $1,000 note. It seems illogical from an economic standpoint for the company to report a gain simply by replacing a 10 percent note with a higher (11 percent) interest note. Because of another quirk in GAAP, however, this transaction would indeed result in an accounting gain. The accounting entry would be:

Decrease:	Old Debt	1,000	
Decrease:	Cash		750
Increase:	Gain		250

Don't Be Fooled by "Profits" from Retiring Debt. Investors and lenders should be concerned when a substantial portion of a company's profit results from one-time gains rather than from normal operating activities. Gains related to the early extinguishment of debt clearly have nothing to do with usual recurring operations. Such gains are sometimes so large, however, that they can dwarf the reported results from operating activities. That's what happened a few years ago at General Host. It reported that net income was *up 300 percent.* A closer review of its statement of operation, however, revealed that its pretax income from continuing operation was actually *down 25 percent.* How could that happen? The answer was quite simple: The company paid off its current debt and replaced it with new, but more expensive debt, resulting in a $17 million gain—thus turning a poor year into a record-breaking one. This decision, however, was shortsighted, because the company's interest expense for future periods increased with the more expensive debt.

Company Profile

General Host

General Host operates the nation's largest chain of specialty
retail stores devoted to the sale of lawn and garden products,
crafts, and Christmas merchandise. It operates 279 stores
under the Frank's Nursery and Crafts and Flower Time trade
names. General Host generates approximately $500 million in
revenue, which increased at 9 percent between 1988 and 1991.
Valued at $450 million in 1986, the company had slumped
badly to only $150 million by mid-1992. See Fig. 5-3.

Technique No. 3: Failing to Segregate Unusual and Nonrecurring Gains or Losses from Recurring Income

As we saw with The Charter Company and General Host, whenever a company has one-time income, GAAP requires that it be
separated on the financial statements from income that stemmed
from ordinary continuing operations. A shenanigan buster
should be particularly alert when nonoperating gains are included with operating (sales) revenue or when noncontinuing (one-
time) gains are included with continuing (recurring) activity.

**Adjust for the Mixing of Gains from Recurring and
Nonrecurring Activities.** One important lesson that might be
learned from studying The Charter Company's financial statement
is the importance of evaluating companies based on their usual and
recurring operations. Income from unusual, one-time activities
should be removed from net income when analyzing a company's
performance and comparing it from one year to the next.
Specifically, the sale of an asset such as real estate or a subsidiary
(assuming that it has increased in value) would result in a company reporting a one-time gain that appears on the income statement
separate from operating income. An investor who fails to examine
the company's operating income (a true measure of how the company has performed) might have the mistaken impression that the
company's earnings are higher than they would otherwise be.

Some companies, such as hotel operator Prime Motor Inns, sell
property every year. Prime, which filed for bankruptcy in late

General Host
Stock Price Movement 1984–1990

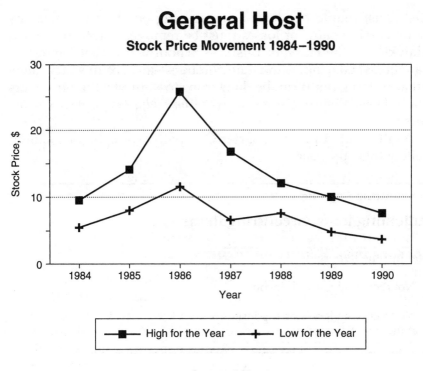

General Host

Year	Price High	Low
1984	$ 9.63	$ 5.43
1985	$14.38	$ 7.50
1986	$25.63	$11.75
1987	$16.38	$ 6.63
1988	$11.75	$ 7.88
1989	$10.00	$ 5.50
1990	$ 7.50	$ 3.88

Fig. 5-3.

1990, claimed that such sales were part of its normal operations, so that they should not be treated as a nonrecurring item. The investor should recognize that Prime's method of accounting for its sales of assets is more aggressive than that used by other companies in its industry. (A company profile of Prime Motor Inns appears in Chapter 10.)

How Can Investors Adjust for Unusual Items? The "bottom line," rather than serving as the entire basis of one's investment

decisions, should be viewed as a starting point from which any
nonrecurring gains or losses must be removed. Professor David
Hawkins of the Harvard Business School warns that "investors
cannot just take the bottom line numbers—and assume they know
what is going on. It can be dangerous to your wealth." Investors
✓ should base their decisions on *net income adjusted for nonrecurring
items*.

As illustrated in The Charter Company example, one should
follow this approach:

Accounting Capsule

Adjusting for Nonrecurring Items

Net Income Reported
Subtract:
  Nonrecurring gains or income
Add:
  Nonrecurring losses or expenses
Net Income Adjusted

Thus, knowledgeable investors temper their excitement over a
big increase in profit if it represents a one-time boost. That was
the reaction by investors in 1986 when Time, Inc., reported $376
million in net income, up 89 percent from the previous year. A
closer look revealed that the comparison with 1985 was incomplete and potentially misleading. For instance, Time sold 20 percent of its cable TV subsidiary in 1986, posting a pretax gain of
$318 million (with Time reporting the gain as operating income).
Time also posted a $33 million pretax gain on another investment
and $113 million in one-time expenses from relocating offices and
reducing staff. By eliminating these one-time gains, Time's after-
tax operating earnings would have been $129 million in 1986—
down 35 percent from 1985.

**Watch for the Mingling of Operating With Nonoperating
Income.**   Besides watching for nonrecurring gains that have
"sneaked" into operations, investors should gauge how much a

company earned from operating activity and how much from ancillary services, such as interest and rental income. When a disproportionate amount comes from ancillary sources, investors should be concerned. Understandably, investors in Cineplex Odeon were perplexed when the company co-mingled all of its revenue in 1989 and labeled it "operating." A substantial portion of its "operating" income had been generated from selling off assets and recording the gain on the sales as operating income. In 1988, $48 million of Cineplex's pretax operating income came from selling its interest in a production company and reporting that gain in the operating revenue section as "Distribution, post production and other." Alert investors who noted this gimmick immediately subtracted these nonrecurring items and found that the company actually had an operating loss of $14.5 million rather than the reported $44 million gain!

Accounting Capsule

Operating versus Nonoperating Income

Operating income	Nonoperating income
Sales revenue	Gain from sale of assets
Service revenue	Investment income

Company Profile

Cineplex Odeon

Cineplex's operating income was overstated because it mingled gains from selling assets with its sales revenue.

Cineplex Odeon operates motion picture theaters in North America, with 1,678 screens in 402 locations. In 1989, the company was worth $1.3 billion. However, its decision to include $48 million of nonoperating income with its operating profits misled investors into thinking that operations were healthy. Cineplex became unprofitable in 1991, and its market value dropped to $270 million. See Fig. 5-4.

Cineplex Odeon

Stock Price Movement 1987–1991

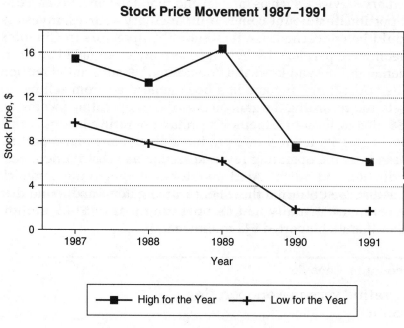

Cineplex Odeon

Year	Price High	Low
1987	$15.63	$9.50
1988	$13.13	$7.75
1989	$16.38	$6.38
1990	$ 7.50	$1.88
1991	$ 6.13	$1.75

Fig. 5-4.

Technique No. 4: Burying Losses under Noncontinuing Operations

Besides watching for nonrecurring and nonoperating transactions, investors and lenders should search for gains or losses from "noncontinuing" activities. Noncontinuing activities, which appear in a separate section at the bottom of the statement of operation, include (1) discontinued operations, (2) extraordinary gains or losses, and (3) the cumulative effect on income of changing accounting principles.

Accounting Capsule

Continuing versus Noncontinuing Income (Loss)

Continuing	Noncontinuing
Operating income	Income (loss) from discontinued unit
Investment income	Extraordinary gain (loss)
Restructuring costs	Cumulative effect of accounting change

Be Alert for Companies Hiding Losses as "Noncontinuing." Companies sometimes try to bury or hide operating losses under "noncontinuing" operations—a violation of GAAP. By shifting these expenses from operations, operating profits are overstated. One company that used this trick was Primerica Corporation, a financial service supplier. In June 1987, Primerica bought the brokerage firm Smith Barney. Several months later came the October stock market crash, when Smith Barney sustained heavy losses. But you would never know that from the unaudited 1987 results for Primerica. Net income for the year was down only slightly, as the company reported big gains on discontinued operations from the previous year. Primerica's 1987 net income on continuing operations, by contrast, was up 43 percent. But what about the well-publicized $61 million bath Smith Barney took on its arbitrage business during the October crash? Primerica buried that little embarrassment in a footnote on "nonrecurring items." Had the $61 million filtered through to continuing operations (as required by GAAP), earnings from continuing operations would have looked anemic. The validity of Primerica's actions is belied by analyst Thornton O'glove's comment that "arbitrage losses are part and parcel of the brokerage business."

6

Shenanigan No. 4: Shifting Current Expenses to a Later Period

The summer of 1991 was filled with excitement and speculation over which city would be granted a National League baseball franchise. The six finalists (Miami, Tampa, Orlando, Denver, Buffalo, and Washington, D.C.) worked hard to convince wealthy individuals of the economic rewards of owning a franchise. Fans in my hometown were disappointed when it was reported that several wealthy Washingtonians, who had considered investing in a baseball franchise, questioned its financial viability and declined to make an offer. They cited the $95 million franchise fee, the cost of signing players, and the short careers of players.

In evaluating the expected profitability of a franchise, the potential investors had to forecast revenues and expenses. The sources of revenue were mainly from ticket receipts, concessions, television contracts, and merchandise sales and licensing. Out-of-pocket expenses included salaries and facilities maintenance; and non-out-of-pocket expenses included principally amortization of the franchise fee and depreciation of player contracts. Because of the flexibility allowed in choosing the time horizon for amortization and depreciation, as well as the tremendous variability in potential expenses that might result from those choices, it became clear to me that the accounting policy decision alone might represent the difference between projecting a profitable and an unprofitable franchise. Consider the following example.

Accounting Capsule

Computing Profits from Owning a Franchise

Assume that estimated revenue is $30 million and estimated out-of-pocket costs are $20 million. Further, the franchise fee of $95 million is amortized over 20 years and player contracts of $24 million are depreciated over 10 years.
The estimated profit (loss) in millions would be:

Estimated revenue		$30.00
Out-of-pocket costs	$20.00	
Amortization costs	4.75	
Depreciation costs	2.40	
Estimated costs		27.15
Estimated profit (loss)		$ 2.85

If, instead, the franchise fee were amortized over 10 years and player contracts were depreciated over 5 years, an investor would conclude that owning a franchise would be unprofitable.
The estimated profit (loss) would be:

Estimated revenue		$30.00
Out-of-pocket costs	$20.00	
Amortization costs	9.50	
Depreciation costs	4.80	
Estimated costs		34.30
Estimated profit (loss)		−$ 4.30

Just as potential investors considering the merits of owning a baseball franchise must evaluate costs and amortization periods, all businesses make such judgments. Managers must make many important and subjective decisions concerning issues such as whether to capitalize or expense costs, the length of time used to amortize costs, and whether to write off permanently impaired assets. This chapter describes several guiding principles related to accounting for assets and expenses and illustrates techniques used by management that violate those principles. Each technique boosts profits by improperly shifting expenses from the current period to a later one.

Shenanigan No. 4: Shifting Current Expenses to a Later Period

Shifting expenses to a later period is one of the most common ways of boosting current-year profits. (The other common approach, discussed in Chapter 3, is to front-end-load revenue.) There are three major techniques used to shift expenses from the current period to a later one: improperly capitalizing costs, amortizing costs too slowly, and failing to write off worthless assets.

How It's Done

1. Improperly capitalizing costs
2. Depreciating or amortizing costs too slowly
3. Failing to write off worthless assets

Technique No. 1: Improperly Capitalizing Costs

Guiding principle: An enterprise should capitalize costs incurred that produce a future benefit and expense those that produce no such benefit.

When a company improperly capitalizes costs (i.e., classifies such costs as an asset rather than an expense), it shifts current-year expenses to a later period. The types of costs that companies sometimes capitalize improperly include start-up costs, research and development costs, advertising, and administrative costs.

Accounting Capsule

Capitalizing and Expensing Costs

Assets represent the economic resources (costs) of an enterprise that are expected to provide some benefit for it beyond the current year. Expenses, in contrast, represent costs that are not expected to provide a future benefit.

Assume that a company improperly capitalizes $100,000 of start-up costs as part of its inventory. In that case, the costs would be charged as an expense when the inventory is sold, perhaps in the following year. The effect is to overstate the current period's profit and to understate next year's profit.

	Incorrect Entry to Record Start-up Costs	
Increase:	Inventory 100,000	
Decrease:	Cash	100,000
	Resulting Entry When Inventory Is Sold the Following Year	
Increase	Expense 100,000	
Decrease	Inventory	100,000

These entries, naturally, are incorrect. The correct entry for recording start-up costs is as follows:

Increase:	Expense 100,000	
Decrease:	Cash	100,000

Watch for the Capitalization of Start-up Costs. A classic example of a company improperly capitalizing start-up costs is defense contractor Lockheed's accounting of its Tri-Star jet program.

Lockheed's Ill-Fated Tri-Star Program

During the early 1970s, Lockheed had to decide whether to continue capitalizing start-up costs related to the development of a new aircraft, the TriStar L-1011, or to write off those costs. The accounting method used for the planes was the "program method": Each plane in the program (300 were envisaged) was to be assigned a presumed average cost, regardless of the actual production costs; any costs incurred in excess of the assigned costs would be deferred until the learning curve took on a favorable slope, so that subsequent costs incurred on a particular plane would be less than the average (thereby permitting the absorption of the previously deferred costs). In theory, this sounds fine—unless, of course, the incremental cost per plane always exceeds the incremental revenue. Unfortunately for Lockheed, this was their fate.

By late 1975, the company had accumulated approximately $500 million in an asset account, while the ill-fated TriStar program showed no signs of profitability. The handwriting was on the wall, however, and Lockheed began writing off the half-billion dollar "blob." But they did so on an installment plan, at the rate of $50 million annually (even though Lockheed continued to have staggering losses on the TriStar program).

Results of Lockheed's Tri-Star Program

	Losses (in millions)
1975	$ 94
1976	125
1977	120
1978	119
1979	188
1980	199
1981	129
Total	$974

Lockheed continued to include the $500 million "development cost" as an asset, net of its annual $50 million amortization, as the losses mounted to almost $1 billion. Clearly, all evidence indicated that the asset was impaired and thus should have been written off in its entirety.

Finally, by the end of 1981, Lockheed wrote off about $400 million after taxes (representing $730 million before taxes, which had previously been reported as an asset). By delaying its decision to write off the asset until 1981, Lockheed probably overstated its profits in the previous years.

Consider the Propriety of Capitalizing R&D Costs. Another common method used to transfer some costs from the statement of operation (where they are shown as an expense) to the balance sheet (where they are shown as an asset) is the capitalization of research and development (R&D) costs. Unfortunately, though, this is in most cases a clear violation of GAAP.

During the early 1980s, for instance, Savin Corporation violated GAAP by classifying $42 million of research and development costs as an asset rather than as an expense in the year incurred. As a result of this improper accounting, Savin overstated its assets and net worth for the fiscal years ended April 1981, 1982, 1983, and 1984, respectively, by approximately $3 million, $12 million, $38 million, and $44 million; it understated its reported losses for those periods by $3 million (50 percent), $9 million (22 percent), $26 million (55 percent), and $7 million (10 percent).

Company Profile

Savin Corporation

Savin was charged by the SEC with overstating its profits by improperly capitalizing research and development costs, thus shifting that expense to a future period.

Savin, an office equipment manufacturer, is engaged in the distribution of copiers, facsimile products, and related supplies and maintenance. It was growing rapidly during the early 1980s, with a market value of $250 million in 1981. The SEC, however, charged that Savin's financial statements for 1981–1985 were false and misleading, causing investors to lose confidence in the company. As a result, the stock price plummeted; by 1992, the company's stock was worthless. See Fig. 6-1.

Look for Companies That Capitalize Advertising.   Another big expense that companies would love to move to the balance sheet is advertising. Imagine how that would boost sagging profits. Some companies, though, do more than imagine.

In 1988, L.A. Gear boosted its income by capitalizing advertising—helping its profits to soar 377 percent over the previous year. This torrid growth continued in the first three months of fiscal 1989 as net income nearly tripled over the 1988 period. Of the total $7.2 million of advertising for the first quarter, it had deferred $3.9 million and expensed only $3.3 million. Had L.A. Gear expensed all the money spent on advertising (as it should have), earnings would have increased only 67 percent rather than

Savin Corporation

Stock Price Movement 1980–1990

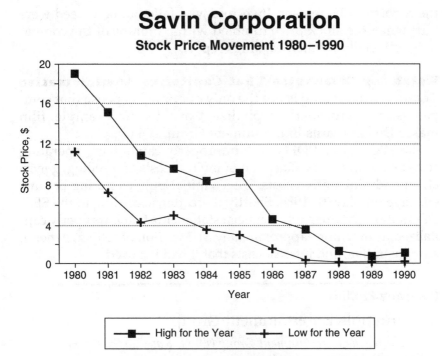

Savin Corporation

Price

Year	High	Low
1980	$19.00	$11.38
1881	$15.25	$ 7.00
1982	$10.88	$ 4.38
1883	$ 9.75	$ 5.00
1984	$ 8.13	$ 3.63
1985	$ 9.13	$ 3.00
1986	$ 4.50	$ 1.63
1987	$ 3.75	$ 0.13
1988	$ 0.94	$ 0.05
1989	$ 0.56	$ 0.09
1990	$ 0.69	$ 0.06

Fig. 6-1.

the reported 195 percent. Investors who failed to take heed were hurt when the stock price tumbled within months of the company's artificially inflated earnings report.

Watch for Companies That Capitalize Administrative Costs. Advertising is not the only operating expense that companies may improperly capitalize. Consider, for example, film maker De Laurentiis Entertainment Group (DEG).

The SEC charged DEG with improperly capitalizing operating costs as a result of its allocation of interest costs and selling, general, and administrative costs. DEG's initial public offering became effective on May 31, 1986. Shortly thereafter, according to the SEC, DEG submitted quarterly financial statements that improperly capitalized as inventory approximately $1.3 million of selling, general, administrative, and interest costs that it had incurred.

Company Profile

De Laurentiis Entertainment Group

> *De Laurentiis Entertainment Group (DEG) was charged by the SEC with improperly capitalizing various operating and administrative costs, thus boosting the current year's profits.*

DEG financed, produced, and distributed motion pictures until it ran into trouble during the late 1980s. In 1987, the government filed suit against DEG, charging that the company had filed false and misleading financial statements for 1983–1986. DEG agreed to settle the case (without admitting or denying any guilt) by submitting an offer of settlement, requiring the company to prepare and adhere to new written internal control policies. See Fig. 6-2.

Technique No. 2: Depreciating or Amortizing Costs Too Slowly

Guiding principle: As an enterprise realizes the benefit from using an asset, the asset or a part thereof should be written off as an expense of the period.

As an enterprise realizes the benefit from using an asset, the expired portion of the asset must be transferred to an expense

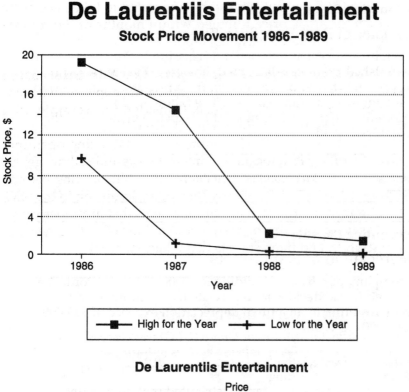

De Laurentiis Entertainment
Stock Price Movement 1986–1989

De Laurentiis Entertainment

Year	Price High	Low
1986	$19.25	$9.63
1987	$14.25	$0.75
1988	$ 1.75	$0.13
1989	$ 0.88	$0.06

Fig. 6-2.

account; and the asset account, of course, must be decreased by a similar amount. This is a common and natural process: A company acquires resources to produce benefits (i.e., to help it generate additional revenue and profits); over time, those resources are used in the productive process, and revenue and profits are realized. At that point, a portion of the assets should be transferred to the appropriate expense accounts. This general principle applies both to inventory that is sold and to plant and equipment (and other assets) that are used in the production process.

Accounting Capsule

Transfer of Past Benefit to Expense

When inventory is purchased, it is classified as an asset. When the finished product is later sold, however, the entire cost of the product should be transferred from inventory (an asset) to cost of goods sold (an expense). The following entry represents the transfer from asset to expense made when the inventory is sold.

Increase:	Cost of Goods Sold	500	
Decrease:	Merchandise Inventory		500

Accounting Capsule

Depreciation of Plant Assets

A company purchases a building for $500,000 and records it as an asset. It also decides to depreciate the building over 25 years, resulting in an annual depreciation expense of $20,000 ($500,000/25 years).

Increase:	Depreciation Expense	20,000	
Decrease:	Building		20,000

At this point, the company shows a building on the balance sheet with a book value of $480,000 ($500,000 − $20,000) and a depreciation expense of $20,000.

Instead, it might have chosen to depreciate the building over a longer period—say, 50 years—to slow down the amortization. The result would be an annual depreciation expense of $10,000 ($500,000/50 years).

Increase:	Depreciation Expense	10,000	
Decrease:	Building		10,000

As a result of the slower depreciation, the building would have a higher book value on the balance sheet and net income would be higher in each of the next 25 years than it would otherwise be (although net income would be lower during years 26 through 50).

While GAAP encourage companies to write off costs quickly as benefits are received, managers have several motivations for writing off assets slowly. First, slow depreciation or amortization keeps assets on the balance sheet longer, resulting in a higher net worth; and second, with slow amortization, expenses are lower and profits higher. Consider the second example on page 86.

Several methods are used to write off assets too slowly, including: depreciating fixed assets too slowly; choosing too long an amortization period for intangible assets or leasehold improvements; amortizing inventory costs too slowly; and increasing the depreciable or amortizable life of an asset.

Question Companies That Depreciate Fixed Assets Too Slowly. By comparing depreciation policies with industry norms, readers can determine whether a company is writing off assets over an appropriate time span. Investors and lenders should be concerned when a company writes off fixed assets too slowly, especially in industries experiencing rapid technological advances. Companies that are slow to modernize will be stuck with outmoded equipment.

That's what happened to Bethlehem Steel in 1977, when stockholders were stunned by the company's $750 million write-off of its vast, but outdated, Lackawanna, New York, mills. The company had failed to use conservative accounting methods in depreciating its plant assets and had failed to consider the replacement cost in the preceding years.

According to accounting analyst Lee J. Seidler of Bear Stearns, "had the steel industry depreciated its plant on a replacement cost basis rather than on historical cost, some of the companies would have been in the red during recent years." For example, U.S. Steel reported earnings in 1973 of $367 million; on a replacement basis, though, *it would have lost $374 million.*

Be Alert for Overly Long Amortization Periods for Intangibles and Leasehold Improvements. As with depreciation, the longer the period over which a company amortizes its intangible assets or its leasehold improvements, the higher will be its earnings during the early years. One should be wary of companies that amortize intangible assets or leasehold improvements over too long a period.

Investors in Cineplex Odeon, the movie theater chain, should have questioned the company's policy of amortizing leasehold improvements, such as seats and carpeting, over an average of 27 years—an unrealistically rosy estimate of these assets' actual life. That overly aggressive accounting practice overstated Cineplex's "true" earnings. Had it amortized the leasehold improvements over a more conservative 15 years, as competitor Carmike Cinemas had done, its net income in 1988 would have been cut by 65 percent to only 54 cents per share.

Accounting Capsule

Amortization of Intangibles

Intangible assets are resources, such as organization costs, trademarks, patents, copyrights, and goodwill, that have value but no physical substance. These assets derive their value from special rights and privileges that accrue to the company owning them. A patent, for example, gives its owner exclusive rights to manufacture, sell, or use an invention or process for 17 years.

The cost of intangible assets, in general, must be written off over their estimated useful lives in a manner similar to depreciation. However, no intangible asset should be written off for more than a 40-year period; in fact, companies using more conservative accounting policies write them off over a shorter period.

Accounting Capsule

Amortization of Leasehold Improvements

A leasehold is a contractual understanding between a lessor and lessee that grants the lessee the right to use specific property for a specified period. If the lessee improves the property, the improvements become the property of the lessor when the lease expires. The lessee should charge the cost of the facilities to the Leasehold Improvements account and amortize the cost over either the remaining life of the lease or the useful life of the improvements, whichever is shorter.

Watch for the Slow Amortization of Inventory Costs. In most industries, the process of writing off inventory is uncomplicated. When a sale takes place, inventory is transferred to an expense: cost of goods sold. In certain businesses, though, determining when and how much inventory to expense is difficult.

In the film business, for example, the costs of making movies or TV programs are capitalized before their release. These costs are then matched (charged as expense) against revenue based on the receipt of revenue. Since such revenue might be realized over several years, however, a company must project the number of years of anticipated revenue flow. By choosing too long a period, the inventory and profits will be overstated.

Take a film that costs $20 million. If the company assumed that revenue would be received over two years, it would expense $10 million each year. If, instead, it assumed that revenues would come in over four years, it would expense $5 million each year. As a result, profits would be $5 million more each year. If the film were a bust, on the other hand, the entire cost should be written off immediately.

Unfortunately, several filmmakers have chosen overly long amortization periods and have failed to write off losing films. Examples include Cannon Group and Orion Pictures.

Cannon Group. The SEC charged that, by overestimating its 1985 film revenue, Cannon was writing off its inventory (unamortized film costs) much too slowly. The result was that Cannon's assets were materially overstated, and its expenses for that year were understated.

Company Profile

Cannon Group

Cannon Group was charged by the SEC with overstating its profits by writing off its film inventory costs too slowly.

Cannon Group (whose name has since been changed to MGM-Pathe Communication Corporation) finances, produces, and distributes motion pictures. By overstating profits in 1983–1986, the company's stock price likewise was also overstated, resulting in a market value of $270 million in 1986. During the early 1990s, the company has been unprofitable, posting a loss of $100 million on sales of $525 million in 1990. In mid-1992 MGM-Pathe was worth $80 million. See Fig. 6-3.

Cannon Group
Stock Price Movement 1984–1991

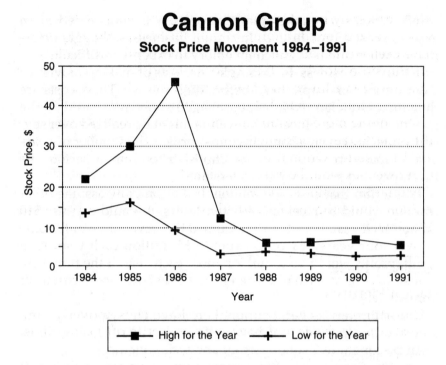

Cannon Group

	Price	
Year	High	Low
1984	$22.00	$13.75
1985	$30.00	$16.50
1986	$45.50	$ 9.50
1987	$13.00	$ 2.63
1988	$ 5.00	$ 3.00
1989	$ 5.50	$ 2.63
1990	$ 6.38	$ 2.25
1991	$ 4.13	$ 2.25

Fig. 6-3.

Orion Pictures. Orion Pictures also had difficulty estimating future revenue (and consequently amortized its film costs too slowly). Further, it was slow in writing off failed films—in some cases waiting years before doing so. In 1985, for example, Orion posted a $32 million loss—half of it resulting from the write-off of 40 films released since 1982. Clearly, these losses were not all from 1985; on the contrary, they represented the residual from Orion's fictitious reporting of profits in the prior years.

More recently, in an October 1991 *Wall Street Journal* article, Orion was criticized for continuing to capitalize film costs that should have been written off years ago. In fact, as a result of either writing off films too slowly or failing to write off its "dogs," Orion's unamortized film costs grew so large that they exceeded the amount of total revenue that the company reported in fiscal 1990.

One of the more questionable estimates Orion made related to the projected revenue from its TV syndication rights to the *Cagney and Lacey* series. Orion was amortizing the costs slowly, assuming that revenues would continue for many years and would eventually total $100 million. Unfortunately, revenues topped out at $25 million—meaning that Orion had expensed its inventory costs far too slowly.

Company Profile

Orion Pictures

Orion Pictures has been criticized for overstating its inventory and profits by failing to write off worthless film inventory costs.

Orion finances, produces, and distributes motion pictures and television programs. In 1991, it posted a $63 million loss on revenue of $584 million, and filed for bankruptcy. See Fig. 6-4.

	1991	1990	1989
	(in millions)		
Revenue	$584	$485	$468
Net income	−63	15	13
Inventory	766	666	467

Be Concerned When the Depreciation or Amortization Period Increases. When net income falls short of management's projections, one fairly innocuous way of "finding" additional income is simply to change an assumption related to the depreciation of fixed assets, the amortization of intangibles or leasehold improvements, or the amortization of inventory costs. In some cases management may be justified in changing assumptions, but investors should be wary when changes appear to be designed to boost earnings.

Orion Pictures
Stock Price Movement 1985–1991

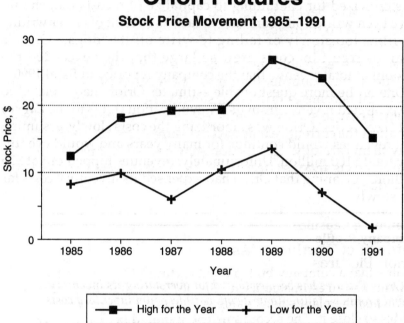

Orion Pictures

Year	Price High	Low
1985	$12.88	$ 8.38
1986	$18.13	$10.00
1987	$19.38	$ 5.50
1988	$19.50	$10.25
1989	$27.00	$14.00
1990	$23.75	$ 6.88
1991	$15.38	$ 1.38

Fig. 6-4.

Technique No. 3: Failing to Write Off Worthless Assets

Guiding principle: When there is a sudden and substantial impairment in an asset's value, the asset should be written off immediately and in its entirety, rather than gradually.

One of the more difficult (and subjective) decisions that management must make is gauging when an asset is "permanently impaired." (In practice, this is often a tough call to make.) Unlike the usual process in which an asset is gradually transferred to an "expense" as a benefit is received, a permanently impaired asset (from which no future benefit will be received) must be abruptly written off as a loss.

If accounts receivable are uncollectible or if investments become worthless, for example, they must be written off. If a piece of equipment becomes worthless, it should also be written off immediately. Because such write-offs are generally large and because they affect the current year as well as future years, investors should study them carefully. This section shows when companies should write off assets and the effect on the financial statements when they fail to do so.

Accounting Capsule

Write-Off of Worthless Assets

Assume that a company built a plant costing $500,000 and that the plant has an estimated useful life of 25 years. Several years later, when the plant's book value is $400,000, the company decides to close it. The accounting entry should be:

Increase:	Loss on Plant Closing	400,000	
Decrease:	Plant and Equipment		400,000

Note two important consequences of the write-off. First, $400,000 will be charged against income this year, rather than $25,000 of depreciation. Second, no depreciation will be charged in future years (compared with the $25,000 that would otherwise have been charged in those years), thus boosting future years' income. Investors should therefore interpret a big write-off as both bad news and good news: Current-year profits will suffer, but the profits in future years will rise. And since the stock market tries to anticipate future profits, the stock price often rises when a company announces a large write-off (as the market might anticipate improved profits in the future).

Watch for Bad Loans and Other Uncollectibles That Have Not Been Written Off. One example of a worthless asset that companies sometimes fail to write off is a loan receivable from a financially distressed client. GAAP require that such receivables be written down to their net realizable value (i.e., the amount a company expects to collect). The process of adjusting the receivables to their net realizable value requires the company to estimate the amount of defaults (or bad debts) and to record a "reserve," or allowance for uncollectibles, that reduces the net receivables. If a company wants to raise its profits, it may simply use a lower estimate of uncollectible receivables. That's precisely what has happened in the banking and casualty insurance industries during the last few years.

Banks must continually estimate what portion of their loans will ultimately go bad and, for such loans, must charge an expense while crediting a reserve. Similarly, property and casualty companies must estimate the amount that they will ultimately pay out on current insurance policies. These amounts are deducted from profits in the year in which they are estimated, not in the year a claim is paid out or a loan becomes worthless. When a loan is written off, the bank removes it from assets and deducts an equal amount from the pool of loss reserves (a bookkeeping entry that does not affect the income statement).

Ideally, the total amount held in reserve should be enough to cover all loans on the books that the bank believes are in default or that will be in default based on conditions that exist at the date of the financial statements. The addition to reserves charged against income each year should be just enough to keep the reserves at the appropriate level. When management fails to reserve a sufficient amount for losses, however, net income and receivables can be substantially overstated.

Several large banks, including the Bank of New England and First Chicago, were charged recently with understating their allowance for loan and lease losses, as well as related provisions for loan and lease losses. As their clients' financial statements deteriorated, the banks should have been increasing the expense (loan loss reserve) and writing off the receivables.

Be Wary of Worthless Investments.   Besides monitoring loans and other receivables to ensure that they are conservatively valued and that they remain so, investments in stocks, bonds, and real estate must be written down as their market value declines and that decline is "other than temporary." This principle is especially significant for certain types of companies, such as insurers,

---

Accounting Capsule

Writing Off Worthless Receivables

Companies are required to present receivables at their net realizable value (i.e., at the amount that they expect to collect). Specifically, a forecast of uncollectible accounts would be subtracted from receivables as follows:

Receivables	$100,000
Less: Allowance for uncollectibles	5,000
Net realizable value	$95,000

The bookkeeping entries involved are as follows:

1. To estimate uncollectible receivables:

Increase:	Bad Debt Expense	5,000	
Increase:	Allowance for Uncollectibles		5,000

2. To write off actual accounts in default:

Decrease:	Allowance for Uncollectibles	2,000	
Decrease:	Accounts Receivable—Joe Deadbeat		2,000

Note that only the first entry—the one estimating uncollectible accounts—affects profits.

---

for whom investments represent a major portion of their assets. Insurance companies are failing in record numbers, yet often with little apparent warning. One reason for the lack of warning is that many insurers carry most of their investments at cost, rather than at their lower market value.

An example of an insurance company that failed to write down its investments was First Executive Life Insurance Corporation, which listed $10 billion in assets at the end of 1990—much of that in junk bonds, whose market value had plunged. In April 1991, regulators seized First Executive Life and its affiliates, stranding thousands of policyholders. It was the biggest insurance failure in American history.

Company Profile

First Executive Life Insurance Corporation

First Executive overstated its profits by failing to write down worthless assets.

First Executive is a California-based insurance holding company. In 1987, it was valued at $200 million. However, like many other insurers who were hurt by declines in real estate and failed to write down losing investments on the balance sheet, it overstated reported net income. In May 1991, First Executive filed for Chapter 11 bankruptcy. See Fig. 6-5.

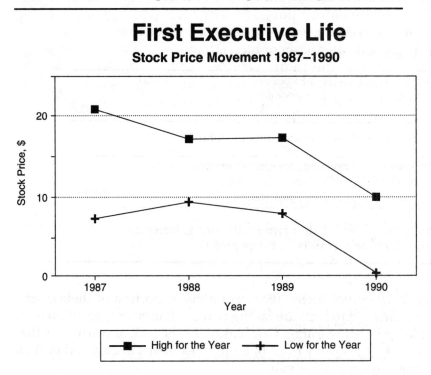

First Executive Life
Stock Price Movement 1987–1990

First Executive Life

Price

Year	High	Low
1987	$20.63	$7.50
1988	$17.00	$9.50
1989	$17.13	$7.88
1990	$ 9.88	$0.13

Fig. 6-5.

7

Shenanigan No. 5: Failing to Record or Disclose All Liabilities

An executive was telling a new secretary what was expected of her. "I want you to be neat, organized, and courteous to all clients," he said. "Above all, I expect you not to gossip about me."

"Oh, yes sir," replied the secretary. "I won't tell anybody anything. You have my total confidence." Then she leaned over the desk and whispered, "Just what is it you've done, sir, that you don't want others to know about?"

When it comes to recording liabilities, some companies share the "less said the better" attitude expressed above. That philosophy results in a policy of disclosing as little as possible about pending lawsuits, long-term purchase commitments, and other potential obligations. Aside from those that should appear on the balance sheet, companies may have many additional obligations that should be disclosed in the footnotes. Investors and lenders should read the financial statements, the accompanying footnotes, and proxy statements to search for a company's total obligations. This chapter describes techniques for uncovering unreported or underreported liabilities.

Shenanigan No. 5: Failing to Record or Disclose All Liabilities

Guiding principle: An enterprise has incurred a liability if it is obligated to make future sacrifices.

Accounting Capsule

Recording Unearned Revenue

A liability represents a present obligation of an enterprise to transfer assets or to provide services to other entities as a result of some past transaction. A common shenanigan is attempting to hide or "keep off the books" actual or probable liabilities. This gimmick is often referred to as "off-balance-sheet financing" (what some consider a close cousin of the "off-budget financing" technique that permits the federal government to exclude many costs from its reported budget).

Companies use four major techniques to keep debt off the books. The first technique is the recording of sales revenue when a company has received cash but has not yet delivered the promised goods or services (i.e., future services are due). The second involves failing to make an entry to accrue expected or contingent liabilities. Both of these techniques result in overstated profits, the first by overstating revenue and the second by understating expenses (or losses). The two other techniques, failing to disclose commitments and contingencies and engaging in transactions to keep debt off the books, are designed to disclose little or nothing about the existence of the obligations.

How It's Done

1. Reporting revenue rather than a liability when cash is received
2. Failing to accrue expected or contingent liabilities
3. Failing to disclose commitments and contingencies
4. Engaging in transactions to keep debt off the books

Technique No. 1: Reporting Revenue Rather Than a Liability When Cash Is Received

Many businesses typically receive cash before they have actually earned it. Franchisers, for example, must often provide continuing services over several years; and airlines reward frequent flyers with free trips and other gifts. When franchisers or airlines fail to defer revenue until it has been earned, profits are overstated, and the financial statements are misleading.

In July and August 1991, my family vacationed in the Orient, the western United States, and Canada. (In fact, a substantial portion of this book was written on planes and at airports during this period.) During our long flight home, I began thinking about how much money airlines must be losing if families like ours can fly all summer to Asia, Hawaii, and Canada for free. Indeed, in a recent quarter, the largest U.S. airlines reported combined losses of over $1 billion.

To understand the current woes and the "generosity" of airlines today, it is important to go back a few years. Starting in 1987 and 1988, airlines sought to entice passengers to fly more frequently and to increase loyalty among their customers by offering double or triple "frequent flyer" points. As a result, frequent flyers began accumulating substantial points for future free flights; and airlines began accumulating substantial future obligations to these passengers. For example, in 1988, I accumulated substantial frequent flyer points. On one trip to Seattle, I earned 18,000 points on Continental Airlines. Since 20,000 points were needed for a free flight, my trip almost qualified for another trip—on the house. Continental, like virtually all other major airlines at that time, was filling its planes with paying customers and boosting revenues—but mortgaging the future.

Although Continental received $300 in revenue for my ticket to Seattle, did the airline really earn that full amount? Absolutely not! In effect, Continental earned only half that amount, since I was entitled to a free trip (which the airline provided in 1991). That's right: Only $150 was earned revenue; the other $150 was "unearned revenue," a liability. Did Continental (or any other airline) record only half the revenue and set up a liability for the other half? Not a chance: GAAP lack any specific guidelines requiring airlines to defer revenue related to frequent flyer commitments. As a result, airlines decide how much, if any, of the *"liability for future free flights"* will be shown as a liability on the balance sheet.

Accounting Capsule

Recording Airline Revenue

	Correct Entry		
Increase:	Cash	300	
Increase:	Unearned revenue		150
Increase:	Revenue		150

	Incorrect Entry		
Increase:	Cash	300	
Increase:	Revenue		300

Not surprisingly, airlines have chosen to accrue only a small fraction of the massive obligation as a liability. For example, an airline analyst at Salomon Bros. estimated in 1988 that the cumulative loss in revenue from triple mileage programs could exceed $940 million.

Carrier	Potential revenue loss (millions)
American Airlines	$190
Continental/Eastern	170
Delta Airlines	140
Northwest Airlines	90
Pan American Airlines	30
Trans World Airlines	15
United Airlines	215
USAir	90
Total	$940

As is illustrated by the recording of airline revenue, deciding what portion is earned and what portion represents a future obligation can be problematical. Although GAAP offer general guidance, interpretation of the specific facts is left to management. And unfortunately, management often has a bias to understate or hide liabilities from investors and lenders. While the meaning and interpretations of revenue and liability appear clear and unambiguous in theory, many companies have difficulty separating the two in practice. For instance, when a company receives payment from a customer, the following question must be asked to determine whether to record that payment as revenue or as a liability: "Was this payment received in exchange for services that *we have already provided*, for which *we have no additional responsibilities*, and for which *the benefits (and risks) of ownership have already passed* to the buyer?" In short: "Has the payment *been earned?*" If the answer is yes, then revenue should be recorded; otherwise, a liability must be recorded.

Ascertain That Cash Received Has Been Earned.   Besides setting up a liability for businesses that earn revenue over time (such as airlines and franchisers), a liability should be recorded if the "risks or benefits" have not passed to the seller. As argued in Chapter 4, when important contingencies (such as uncollectibility or possible returns and/or cancellations) still exist, no revenue should be recorded. Rather, a liability must be shown on the balance sheet. Thus, if a company records revenue while such contingencies exist, revenue and profits have been overstated and liabilities understated.

Consider the decision of Seattle-based Thousand Trails, a pioneer in the private-membership campground resort industry, to record revenue at the time new members signed up. The members paid virtually no money down; nearly 90 percent financed payments through the company; and many new members canceled within days of signing up. Moreover, neither a credit rating nor a bank account was required to qualify for membership. With such risks, it's hard to imagine how Thousand Trails justified its practice of recognizing up front the entire amount received as revenue.

Sure enough, as customers stopped paying and walked away from signed contracts, the company started experiencing serious financial difficulties. Unfortunately, when the story of its accounting gimmicks finally broke (in the form of a November 1984 *Wall Street Journal* article), it was too late to help investors. The stock plummeted from $29.50 per share in late 1983 to $5.50 one year later. Third quarter 1985 earnings declined 87 percent from the same period one year earlier.

Company Profile

Thousand Trails

Thousand Trails overstated its profits by recording revenues at the point of sale, even though collection from members was uncertain.

Thousand Trails sells membership-based campgrounds featuring family-oriented facilities and activities throughout the United States. Business grew rapidly during the early 1980s, and its market value peaked at $700 million in 1984. When it was reported (in the *Wall Street Journal*) in 1984 that the company was using aggressive accounting methods and was overstating its profits, the stock began a long and sustained decline. More recently, sales dropped off to $80 million, down considerably from a 1986 high of $113 million. Thousand Trails was worth only $23 million in mid-1992. See Fig. 7-1.

Technique No. 2: Failing to Accrue Expected or Contingent Liabilities

The second approach for keeping debt off the books is failing to accrue a loss or an expected obligation. Losses should be accrued for expected payments related to litigation, tax disputes, and so forth. GAAP require that companies accrue a loss when two conditions are both present: (1) There is a probable loss, and (2) the amount can be reasonably estimated.

Accounting Capsule

Estimating a Loss Contingency

When both requirements for a contingent loss have been met, a loss should be accrued. For instance, assume that a company is about to lose in litigation and almost certainly will have to pay out $6,000. Since both conditions for accruing the loss are present, the following entry should be made.

Increase:	Loss from Litigation	6,000	
Increase:	Estimated Liability		6,000

Recording this transaction increases liabilities and reduces net income. Conversely, failing to record the entry would overstate profits.

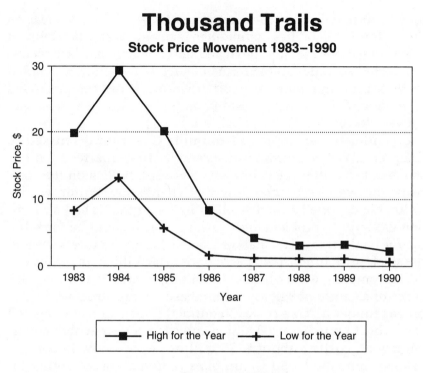

Thousand Trails
Stock Price Movement 1983–1990

Thousand Trails

Year	Price High	Low
1983	$19.80	$ 8.63
1984	$29.50	$12.88
1985	$20.13	$ 5.50
1986	$ 8.38	$ 1.75
1987	$ 4.00	$ 1.13
1988	$ 2.63	$ 1.13
1989	$ 2.75	$ 1.20
1990	$ 2.00	$ 0.75

Fig. 7-1.

Technique No. 3: Failing to Disclose Commitments and Contingencies

As we all know, existing obligations from past transactions must be reported as liabilities, with a corresponding charge to an expense. Further, GAAP require that contingent liabilities be accrued in some circumstances. What about future commitments or contingencies that companies have? For instance, a company may have a long-term rental or purchase agreement. GAAP are less clear on these "future" liabilities, giving management greater flexibility. If these obligations are substantial and the company may be adversely affected by unfavorable terms in such agreements, a detailed footnote is the minimum required disclosure. When companies fail to provide all the details, investors and financial analysts must read between the lines to learn the full story.

Consider the example of Columbia Gas, first discussed in Chapter 2. When Columbia released its first-quarter financial statements for 1991, most analysts were still bullish on the company and were recommending that clients buy. Within weeks, Columbia dropped a bombshell—disclosing that it had a $1 billion gas supply problem and warning that it could be forced to file for bankruptcy. The market reacted quickly to this news and the stock price tumbled 40 percent, or $700 million, in one day.

The company was criticized for failing to highlight the significance of a future obligation to purchase a large amount of natural gas (under a "take or pay" contract). This contract obligated Columbia to purchase 200 billion cubic feet a year at above-market prices, costing about $125 million. As we now know, gas prices plummeted, and Columbia's customers were opting for cheaper fuel. While Columbia had to live up to its commitments to producers, its utility customers were free to buy gas from the cheapest source.

Probe for a Troubled Company with Fixed Payments. Many other companies have similar long-term commitments, particularly related to leases for facilities. These commitments could become a problem if business deteriorates and a company cuts back its operations. Such long-term commitments proved to be a major problem for computer vendor Businessland in early 1991, when its business declined significantly. Unfortunately, it still had to pay rent on dozens of facilities it no longer occupied and for which it was unable to find tenants (see the example on page 105).

Watch for an Unrecorded Postretirement Liability. Many companies incur huge unrecorded liabilities if they have failed to fund pension or other postretirement funds adequately. Until recently, with the issuance of a new accounting rule on postre-

---

Company Profile

Businessland

Businessland had an unrecorded liability related to a long-term lease of facilities.

Businessland distributes and supports multivendor microcomputer and workstation systems. In 1987 its business was robust, and its market value approached $350 million. More recently, Businessland became unprofitable, posting a loss of $23 million on sales of $1.3 billion. In November 1991, Businessland was acquired by JWP, Inc. See Fig. 7-2.

---

tirement benefits (*SFAS No. 106*), companies generally disclosed nothing about this liability anywhere in their financial statements or in the footnotes. The pension or postretirement expense that is based on this liability, however, must appear on the statement of operation as of 1993.

Accounting Capsule

Transition Rules for *SFAS No. 106*—Postretirement Benefits

Beginning in 1993, companies must start implementing *SFAS No. 106* on postretirement benefits. The most troublesome decision is how to account for the transition costs—the difference between the obligations to which the company has committed and the fair market value of assets that they have to set aside to pay this obligation (in most cases nothing). Companies must choose between immediate and deferred recognition.

Immediate recognition.   As an immediate write-off, the transition amount is recognized in the "noncontinuing" section as "effect of a change in accounting principle" and as a long-term liability. Some companies decided to begin implementation before 1993, using this approach. In 1991, IBM took a $2.3 billion charge against its first-quarter income.

Deferred recognition.   Employers using this approach must write off the transition costs on a straight-line basis over the service life of its employees, but not more than 20 years.

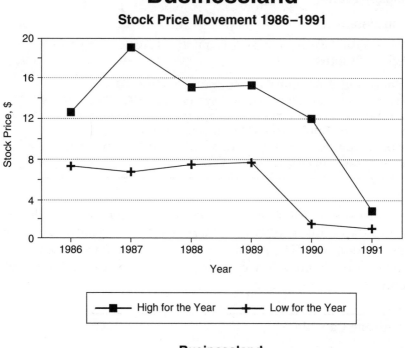

Businessland

Stock Price Movement 1986–1991

Businessland

Year	Price High	Low
1986	$12.50	$7.13
1987	$19.00	$6.50
1988	$15.00	$7.63
1989	$15.25	$7.75
1990	$11.88	$1.13
1991	$ 2.88	$0.88

Fig. 7-2.

Read Debt Covenants Carefully for Contingencies. When a company borrows money, it must often sign a restrictive agreement called a debt covenant. This document is meant to protect the lender if the borrower experiences significant financial difficulties. Among the restrictions are that net worth (owners' equity) and working capital must stay above a certain level. If the borrower violates the terms of its debt covenant, the lender can "call" (i.e., demand immediate payment of) the loan.

Consider the case of one of the Southwest's largest lenders,

Southmark Corporation. In early 1989, with the Texas real estate market in shambles, Southmark was experiencing serious financial difficulties. Its debt covenants included a provision requiring it to maintain a positive stockholders' equity. Unfortunately, a $1.04 billion loss had wiped out Southmark's stockholders' equity; and its 30-day grace period with lenders was about to expire. Moreover, Southmark's debt covenants prevented it from making capital contributions, thereby reducing its regulatory capital to only $10 million. Consequently, the lenders refused to extend additional borrowing, hastening Southmark's eventual demise.

Company Profile

Southmark Corporation

Southmark's poor operating performance placed it in violation of its debt covenant, causing lenders to cut off financing.

Southmark was engaged in the real estate and financial services industries. Its principal business was the management and sale of real estate and the management of real estate partnerships. In 1986, its market value approached $670 million. However, with the slump in the Texas real estate market during the mid- and late 1980s, the company's fortunes also sagged. To avoid being cut off from bank borrowing, Southmark used artificial and cosmetic methods to keep its balance sheet in technical compliance with debt covenants. Finally, in 1990, its luck ran out, and it filed for bankruptcy. See Fig. 7-3.

Technique No. 4: Engaging in Transactions to Keep Debt off the Books

It has been said that most people have three desires in life: food, shelter, and keeping debt off the books. While some may disagree with this aphorism (perhaps changing the order of the three desires), some companies do go to great lengths to keep debt off their balance sheets, and they can use several accounting tricks to make it disappear. In Chapter 6 we showed how managers can make income appear from nowhere. Similarly, some managers have a talent for making debt disappear from the balance sheet. Three ways of causing debt to disappear are: swapping it for

Southmark Corporation

Stock Price Movement 1985–1990

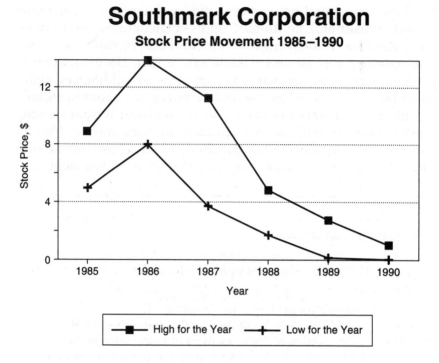

Southmark Corporation

Year	High	Low
	Price	
1985	$ 9.13	$4.90
1986	$14.00	$8.00
1987	$11.25	$3.75
1988	$ 4.88	$1.38
1989	$ 2.38	$0.05
1990	$ 0.69	$0.02

Fig. 7-3.

equity; using a separate subsidiary for borrowing; and using an accounting gimmick known as "defeasance."

Note: Using any of these techniques might understate a company's total debt on the balance sheet; each technique fits into the category of "window dressing" and is not a violation of GAAP.

Examine Any Debt for Equity Swaps.   When the stock market rallied in August 1983, many companies realized that their bondholders might be happier with the suddenly more valuable equity.

From the companies' point of view, this was definitely a chance to have their cake and eat it too. Calling in debentures would wipe away debt from the balance sheet, eliminate interest payments (thus raising earnings), and increase equity. Earnings would be further increased by the difference between the value of the new stock and the face value of the bonds. Naturally, since a company wouldn't pay cash for any of the bonds but would swap equity for them instead, it would pay no tax on the resultant profits.

It was such a good deal that in 1982, Allied Corp. engineered two debt–equity swaps, erasing more than $545 million in debt in the process and increasing its earnings per share by about 20 percent—from $4.98 to $6.22 per share. That same year, U.S. Steel decided to use this new technique to boost its slumping profits and weak balance sheet.

Be Wary of Companies Using Subsidiaries for Borrowing. Another way of keeping the balance sheet free of debt is to set up a separate subsidiary and have the subsidiary borrow the funds. During the early 1970s, home builder Stirling Homex did just that, setting up a subsidiary called U.S. Shelter to provide off-balance-sheet financing for some of Stirling's receivables. Because of Stirling's high debt–equity ratio, it would probably not have been able to obtain more bank loans directly. So the subsidiary served as a perfect vehicle for any additional borrowing. However, the benefit of this gimmick was short-lived: Stirling Homex declared bankruptcy only one year after going public.

During the 1990s, it will be more difficult for a parent to use subsidiaries as vehicles for borrowing (and thus keep debt off the parent's books), because the parent must consolidate balance sheets of all majority-owned subsidiaries (*SFAS No. 94*).

Watch for Defeasance of Debt.   One of the more ingenious ways of making debt disappear came special delivery, courtesy of the FASB in the form of *SFAS No. 76*. For many companies it was a dream come true. It allowed companies to wipe debt off their books without the hassle of a debt swap or the formation of a separate subsidiary.

The approach, known as in-substance defeasance, works like this. A company decides that it wants to clear $20 million of 9 per-

cent bonds off its books. It sets up a trust and irrevocably funds it
with 9 percent U.S. Treasury bonds at the same par value, but
purchased at a discount for $17 million. The interest received on
the government securities has to cover the interest payments on
the debt, and the maturity value of the government securities
must be enough to repay the debt when it comes due. The company records a profit equal to the difference between the book
value of its bonds and the price of the Treasury bonds it buys for
the trust. Here's how it would look on the books:

Accounting Capsule

Recording the Defeasance of Debt

Balance sheet ($ in millions):

Before the defeasance		After the defeasance	
Asset	**Liability**	**Asset**	**Liability**
None	Debt $20	None	None

Journal entry—Purchase security:

Increase:	Investment	17	
Decrease:	Cash		17

Journal entry—Defease debt and place asset in trust:

Decrease:	Debt	20	
Decrease:	Investment		17
Decrease:	Gain		3

The net result of the two journal entries is to remove both the
debt and the investment from the balance sheet. And, as an
added incentive, the company posts a $3 million gain—
without receiving a dime! Moral of the story: Investors seeing
"gain from debt defeasance" on the statement of income
should be skeptical.

Exxon Corporation.   Exxon was one of the "pioneers," using this
technique in 1982 to defease $515 million of debt, report a gain of
$132 million, and improve its debt–equity ratio in one fell swoop.

8

Shenanigan No. 6: Shifting Current Income to a Later Period

I was once hired to audit a local car dealership. During that engagement, I reviewed a schedule showing the cars sold by each salesperson for the entire year. Upon close examination, I noticed an interesting phenomenon: Among the top producers, there were virtually no sales during the last 10 days of most months, and there were abnormally high sales during the first few days of each month. The Sherlock Holmes in me said that something didn't smell right, so I decided to interview the salespeople. After speaking to a few of them, I began to understand the unusual monthly sales pattern. Salespeople receive bonuses based on the number of units sold per month—but with a cap. Once a salesperson reaches the maximum bonus for a given month, he or she has no incentive to sell (or, more precisely, to record a sale) that month. Sure enough, those top salespeople that reached the cap chose to shift sales (and potential bonuses) to the following month. Similarly, companies that have had better-than-expected years might benefit by shifting some income to future years.

Up to this point, we have shown five financial shenanigans, each of which enables companies to overstate their true profits. Not all companies, though, must resort to such tactics. In fact, some companies have profits that far exceed projections and expectations. That situation, however, creates another problem for management: how to maintain such high levels of income in the future. Companies may use two strategies to shift some of today's extraordinarily high profits to a later period. One strategy (discussed in this chapter) involves a technique that shifts *income* to a later accounting period. The other strategy (discussed in Chapter 11) involves techniques that shift future-period *expenses* to the current period.

Shenanigan No. 6: Shifting Current Income to a Later Period

Guiding principle: Revenue should be recorded in the period in which it is earned.

How It's Done

1. Creating reserves to shift sales revenue to a later period

---

Accounting Capsule

Setting up a Reserve

Assume that a company made a cash sale for $900. The correct entry would be:

Increase:	Cash	900	
Increase:	Sales		900

This transaction increases both assets and revenue. An accounting trick used when a company wants to defer some sales revenue until later is to record a liability initially and to wait until the following year to transfer the liability to revenue. This trick, also known as "setting up reserves," shifts income from a year in which a company may have a large profit to a later year when profits are expected to be weaker.

The journal entries to set up and later tap a reserve are as follows. For this year,

Increase:	Cash	600	
Increase:	Unearned Revenue		600

For next year,

Decrease:	Unearned Revenue	200	
Increase:	Sales Revenue		200

The result is that this year's sales revenue is recorded as earned in a later period.

Technique No. 1: Creating Reserves to Shift Sales Revenue to a Later Period

Sometimes companies intentionally understate their profits for the current period rather than overstate them. One shouldn't be misled, however, by their apparent humility or conservatism. On the contrary, companies generally understate their profits only if they will benefit by doing so (e.g., it will enable them to overstate profits in subsequent years).

An example of this strategy is referred to as "smoothing of income." Most executives prefer to report earnings that follow a smooth, regular upward path. They hate to report declines; but they also want to avoid increases that vary wildly from year to year. It's better to have two years of 15 percent earnings than increases of 30 percent one year and none the next. As a result, some companies "bank" earnings by understating them in a particularly good year and then use the reserves in bad years to boost profits.

Many have criticized the use of reserves to smooth income, including former Salomon Bros. CEO John Guttfreund. According to Guttfreund: "[W]hen things are going well executives try to legitimately squirrel away reserves." Those squirreled-away reserves, which reduce reported profits, are kept in the proverbial "corporate sugar bowl." When earnings turn down, managers can reach into the sugar bowl by cutting back the reserve provision for the current year: The lower the reserve, the higher the income.

Smoothing Means Income Manipulation. The use of reserves to shift income to a later period can be as serious an income manipulation ploy as front-end loading of revenue. The effect in each case is to intentionally mislead investors and creditors. By front-end loading revenue, future years' income is recorded in the current year; conversely, by smoothing income, current year's income is shifted to a future period. One result of income smoothing could be that companies that have been profitable for several years would defer part of each year's income by setting up a reserve. Then, when earnings begin to slump, they would tap into the reserves and be able to report consistently high profit over the years.

Smoothing Usually Brings Unpleasant Surprises Later. Although income smoothing (using reserves) arguably is not as common as shenanigans that overstate profits, investors, lenders, and auditors should be equally vigilant in searching for it. Consider the following case. A company has two outstanding years in a row. Expecting a slowdown in business, it sets up a reserve in year 2. In year 3, sales and cash flows decline steeply. The company taps into its reserves, and the financial statements show a healthy profit. Investors and others have been duped and will later be shocked when the company announces plant closings and a severe cash crunch. Had the company reported earnings more faithfully, of course, the plant closings and cash crunch might have been equally unavoidable; but the investors (who are, after all, the *owners* of the company) would have had some advance warning. Another possible scenario, though, is more optimistic: An early warning system allows major investors the time to investigate problems and to work with management to correct them.

But Not Everyone Understands That Smoothing Is Wrong. As shown above, income smoothing sometimes leads to extremely serious consequences. Inexplicably, however, many people find nothing wrong in smoothing. In fact, some boast publicly about their ability to create reserves. Consider Houston-based Allied Bancshares. It had posted 31 quarterly earnings increases before showing a decline in the final quarter of 1983. One of the bank's senior officials, describing the company's use of reserves, stated: "We believe it is entirely appropriate to use high profit opportunities to build special reserves for cycles such as the current one." The bank's treasurer further explained:

> When you are bumping along with such good earnings, you don't get any benefit by showing extraordinary increases. Some years we could have reported extremely higher earnings than we did. In fact we were building our reserves quite high in late 1980 and early 1981.

Auditors Must Also Be More Alert. Independent auditors are responsible for certifying that financial statements are neither false nor misleading. However, they seem to be less concerned when companies intentionally understate profits (using reserves) than when they overstate them. Auditors often wink at reserves as long as companies don't materially misrepresent results. That practice still gives management enormous latitude in matters of judgment.

Be Critical of Successful Companies with Large Reserves. One successful company that held back some of its revenue as a reserve was Daimler-Benz, the maker of the Mercedes automobile. When Benz executives were questioned about the seemingly greater profits of General Motors, the German officials admitted that they use reserves as a "hedge against a downturn" in the auto markets. Thus, by establishing reserves, they have instant profits available to tap when a downturn occurs—as it invariably does in the cyclical auto industry.

Most companies that attempt to defer income simply set up a reserve (as Daimler-Benz did) and tap it when earnings need a boost. H.J. Heinz, however, went much further to trick its shareholders during the 1970s. It was engaged in several activities characterized by the SEC as fraudulent that allowed it to defer income until a later period in order to smooth income. Specifically, at two of its affiliates, Starkist Foods and Heinz USA, employees postdated shipping documents or failed to process them within the related fiscal year, so that products sold at the end of one fiscal year were recorded as sales of the subsequent fiscal year.

Some observers have speculated that the Heinz employees

were driven to these actions by the company's management incentive plan (MIP), which awarded bonuses largely on the basis of the net profit after tax (NPAT)—but only up to a certain level for each year. Once that level was achieved, there was no incentive to show any additional profit that year. Rather, there was an incentive to begin building up an "inventory of profit" for the next year. By holding back income (or prepaying expenses) in good years, when the NPAT goal was already surpassed, managers were creating a "reserve" that could be tapped in bad years.

Public disclosure of its fraudulent financial statements was a serious, but only a temporary, setback for shareholders in Heinz. With new management and a renewed commitment to the integrity of financial reporting, its stock price increased over 1,400 percent during the 1980s.

9

Shenanigan No. 7: Shifting Future Expenses to the Current Period

At an investment seminar I led, one of the participants (whose name was Claude) announced: "The biggest problems facing this country and individuals have been caused by too much borrowing." He went on to explain that the out-of-control deficit and the precipitous rise in both corporate and individual bankruptcies were the result of spending more than you have. Claude was asked about his own investing strategy. He explained: "First, I never borrow when buying a car or other consumer goods; and second, I am trying to pay off the mortgage on my house before buying investments like stocks or bonds." Claude summed up his rather conservative (and, I may add, boring) philosophy by stating, "pay today and party tomorrow."

While Claude's investment approach is clearly far from the mainstream, his philosophy about sacrificing today in order to benefit tomorrow is not unusual. In fact, as we discussed in the last chapter, Heinz and other companies intentionally shifted current income to a later period. Similarly, many companies seek to improve future-period "performance" by shifting expenses from those periods into the current year. This is particularly true when new management attempts to show that a dramatic improvement occurred during its first year on the job. This chapter describes various techniques for boosting current-year expenses (thereby lowering current profits) in order to boost profits in the future.

Shenanigan No. 7: Shifting Future Expenses to the Current Period

Guiding principle: Expenses should be charged against income in the period in which the benefit is received.

Chapter 8 introduced the concept of income smoothing and the use of reserves to shift income to a later accounting period. A company could achieve similar results by prepaying discretionary expenses or writing off future years' amortization of assets (and thereby taking a big bath).

How It's Done

1. Accelerating discretionary expenses into the current period
2. Writing off future years' depreciation or amortization

Technique No. 1: Accelerating Discretionary Expenses into the Current Period

If a company has already met its income projections for the period, it may attempt to shift next year's expenses into the current period. Heinz, in addition to improperly shifting income, was found guilty of prepaying expenses to boost the next year's profit. One of its subsidiaries engaged in other ploys as well, such as misstating its cost of sales and improperly soliciting bills from vendors for advertising and expensing invoices for services that had not yet been received.

Be Alert for Prepayment of Operating Expenses.   In one of the more ingenious moves in recent years, a senior executive at a large New York–based company ordered his subordinates to do whatever they could to incur expenses by the end of the year. Profits were going to be robust no matter what, so he told them it would be wise to save a little for an encore the following year. One middle manager bought $12 million worth of postage metering, an item that could be deducted immediately even though the benefits would endure through millions and millions of letters (at today's postal rate, over 41 million letters).

Be Concerned When the Depreciation or Amortization Period Decreases. In Chapter 6 we illustrated how a company could boost its profits simply by depreciating or amortizing certain assets over a longer period of time. Conversely, if the objective was to defer some of the current year's profits until the future (i.e., shifting expenses into the current period), a company might depreciate fixed assets and amortize intangibles and leasehold improvements over a shorter period of time.

Accounting Capsule

Amortizing Assets

A movie rental store has $100,000 of movies to depreciate. If it assumes a five-year useful life, the annual expense would be $20,000. The amortization entries would be:

Increase:	Depreciation Expense	20,000	
Decrease:	Asset		20,000

If the depreciation period was only two years, however, the annual expense would be $50,000. Thus, assuming a shorter useful life results in lower profits the first few years.

Technique No. 2: Writing off Future Years' Depreciation or Amortization

As shown above, the amortization of assets over a shorter period will accelerate expensing into the first few years. However, the reported performance in future years (i.e., after the depreciation or amortization period ends) will benefit. Taken to the extreme, that approach implies a complete amortization or write-off of the asset during the current year, resulting in a large expense this year and none in future years. Consider the following illustration.

Accounting Capsule

Writing off Worthless Assets

A company is depreciating an asset that cost $400,000 over a 20-year useful life (annual depreciation of $20,000). Early in year 3, the company decides to close the plant and take a big bath. It makes the following entry:

Increase:	Loss on Plant Closing	360,000	
Decrease:	Plant and equipment		360,000

Note two important consequences of the write-off. First, $360,000 rather than $20,000 will be charged against income this year. Second, no depreciation will be charged in future years (compared with the $20,000 that would otherwise have been charged), resulting in a boost for future income. Investors should therefore interpret a big write-off as both bad and good news: This year's profits will be down, but future years' profits will be boosted. And since the stock market tries to predict future profits, a company's announcement of a large write-off often leads investors to anticipate improved profits in the future and therefore to bid up the stock price.

The mechanics might be clear by now, but the logic of writing off an entire asset may be less so. Imagine that you are CEO of a company having an awful year in 1992 because of the recession. You look to the future and realize that a few investments from several years ago are running out of steam. Why not drop all the bad news into one quarter, take a big reduction in profits, and get it behind you? In other words, take a "big bath." It rids the company of excess expenses and may eventually firm up profits.

As you might expect, taking a big bath is controversial. Managers who take the write-off often support their decision by claiming that they are being "conservative." Critics argue, however, that management often should have written off those assets long before it actually did. Because of the questions raised about the timing, size, and intent of such big baths, accounting numbers have lost credibility. Those frustrations were best summed up by Robert Monk and Nell Minow in their book *Power and Accountability* (1991) when they stated:

> At the time of the "big bath," prior period earnings may be reduced, but there is no adverse impact on current or future reported results. This does not seem to be the basis for a discipline imposed by the marketplace. You can believe neither the past nor the future. The figures are virtually meaningless.

Timing the Big Bath. Companies are most likely to take a big bath during particular periods. First, when new managers take over, they are tempted to write off the old projects and assets of their predecessors to show strong improvement during the coming years. Second, when a company has a large nonrecurring gain, it might search for large expenses to charge against it. And third, when earnings are particularly weak, management sees an opportunity to shift additional expenses (which will most likely not even be noticed) to the current period. The benefit, naturally, is that the additional current charges mean fewer charges in the future. To quote Claude, "pay today, party tomorrow."

Ma Bell Takes a Bath. One of the largest write-offs in U.S. corporate history occurred in 1988, when AT&T became convinced that $6.6 billion of its plant assets (which were growing obsolete with the industry's rapid change to fiber optics) were permanently impaired. As a result of the write-off, the company reported a massive loss for the year. AT&T was positioning itself for a rapid improvement in future periods, however, as it effectively shifted $6 billion of expenses from future accounting periods to 1988.

Once again in 1991, AT&T announced a massive charge against income—its fourth since the company's government-mandated breakup in 1984 (with write-offs totaling more than $24 billion). The company announced that it would take a $4 billion charge to absorb its new subsidiary NCR Corporation and to cut big losses in its office phone equipment business. A large portion of these charges related to personnel cuts; AT&T has cut more than 100,000 jobs since its breakup, to a current employment level of 272,000. And how did the stock market react to this news? Its stock price jumped $1.625, and analysts were trumpeting the company's future: "[T]he AT&T ship has finally turned around and is headed in the right direction."

Big Blue Takes a Plunge.   When IBM announced that in the first quarter of 1992 it had a robust profit of $600 million, following a loss of $2.8 billion in 1991, analysts were pleasantly surprised by the "rapid turnaround." These analysts missed the real reason for the improvement, which was shifting billions of dollars of 1992 and later expenses to 1991. By charging costs associated with implementing *SFAS No. 106* on postretirement expenses and severance-pay obligations all in 1991, IBM had shifted large expenses that would otherwise have been charged to future periods to 1991. As a result, 1992 performance was misleadingly strong compared with 1991.

The Tub Is Getting Crowded.   In part because of the recession and the accompanying weak earnings, many companies, including AT&T ($2.6 billion), Occidental Petroleum ($2.0 billion), and Continental Airlines ($1.8 billion), took large write-offs in 1991.

Big Baths Aren't Always Dirty.   While many companies should be criticized for writing off assets too slowly, others should be praised for taking aggressive actions to cut costs when the economy is weak and plant closings and asset write-offs are necessary. The latter was the case in 1991, when many companies prudently fired employees to cut their costs and streamline operations. IBM, for example, announced that it would reduce personnel by 20,000 employees—thereby saving the company hundreds of millions of dollars in future expenses.

10

Cash Is King: Study the Statement of Cash Flows

When I was growing up in the 1950s, things seemed much simpler. Back then, MBAs were about as common as Martians, and businesspeople measured success by how much cash was in the bank at the end of each week. One such businessman was my Uncle Barry, who sold men's slacks in Bensonhurst (a section of Brooklyn, New York). Uncle Barry had a few corny (but true) expressions to describe his own successful business. First, he would say, "buy low and sell high," and second, "always keep track of your cash account."

Lately, I've come to appreciate Uncle Barry's teachings, especially his fixation on cash flows. Indeed, many others, including the former chairman of the SEC, Harold Williams, argue that cash flow data are more valuable than reports of net income. According to Williams, "If I had to make a forced choice between having earnings information and having cash flow information, I would take the latter." The reason is simple: Accounting profit, as reported on the statement of income, is prepared according to accrual accounting rules and therefore might be subject to manipulation; cash flow, on the other hand, is not subject to the intricacies of accrual accounting. Taken alone, cash flow is potentially as misleading as net income. The key point is that the statements must be read as a group, with an understanding of how they interact.

The Cash Flow Statement and CFFO

The statement of cash flows shows the net inflow (or outflow) of cash during the period covered by the statement. Cash flows are presented on this statement in three distinct categories based on the activity that generated them: operations, investments, and financing. (An illustration of a statement of cash flows appears in the tutorial at the end of the book.)

The first section of the statement of cash flows presents the cash flows from operations (CFFO). It measures a company's operating performance on a cash basis. Net income, in contrast, measures operating performance on an accrual basis. While both measures are important to assess a company's performance, each has important limitations. The cash basis ignores sales for which money is due and expenses for which money is owed. Accrual-based net income, however, is a less objective measure, requiring much judgment and, as a result, it can be more subject to manipulations or shenanigans.

Accounting Capsule

Net Income versus CFFO

Net income is the excess of revenue over expenses, computed on an accrual basis (meaning that revenue is recorded when earned, and expenses are charged when incurred).

Cash flow from operations equals the net cash inflows (outflows) from operations. It is computed as follows:

Net income
Plus: Noncash expenses, such as depreciation
Plus (or minus): Changes in operating assets and liabilities

Note: Some analysts use an alternative measure of cash flow, referred to as discretionary cash flow. It is computed as follows: CFFO − Projected capital additions − Dividends − Projected debt retirement.

___

CFFO Measures Quality of Earnings

An excellent way of determining a company's "quality of earnings" is by comparing CFFO (or, alternatively, discretionary cash flow) with reported net income (CFFO/net income). If a healthy net income figure can be validated by a similarly high CFFO, chances are that the net income was truly earned (in the course of business) rather than financially engineered. If, on the other hand, CFFO is negative for several periods while net income is positive, or if the net income is consistently higher than CFFO over a longer time frame, a company might have a poor quality of earnings.

Strong companies typically report healthy profits (i.e., high net income) and generally have significant net inflows of cash from operations; conversely, weak companies typically report small profits or even losses and generally have small net inflows (and sometimes net outflows) of cash from operations. If a company reports healthy profits accompanied by net outflows of cash, though, investors and lenders should be suspicious.

The CFFO/net income comparison is particularly pertinent for well-established companies, whose sales, receivables, and inventory generally don't fluctuate rapidly. Two such companies, retailer W.T. Grant and motel operator Prime Motor Inns, are profiled in this chapter.

Conversely, the CFFO/net income comparison is less applicable to young, profitable, fast-growth companies that must incur substantial costs to fund their growth in receivables and inventory. For example, Cabletron Systems and Cisco Systems—two of the fastest-growing computer companies—had CFFO/net income ratios of significantly less than 1.0 for 1990 and 1991, as shown in the following accounting capsule.

Accounting Capsule

Computing CFFO/Net Income Ratio

| | CFFO | Net income | CFFO/net income |
	(in millions)		ratio
Cabletron Systems			
1991	$23	$36	0.63
1990	6	22	0.27
CISCO Systems			
1991	$ 9	$14	0.64
1990	2	10	0.20

Using Cash Flow Analysis to Predict Bankruptcy

Cash flow analysis, in conjunction with traditional measures of profitability, liquidity, and solvency (discussed in the Tutorial at the end of the book), often provides early warning that a company is in trouble. Some companies might continue to report profits even though cash flows from operations are negative for several years. In extreme cases, such as W.T. Grant and Prime Motor Inns, companies may continue reporting profits even though they are on the verge of declaring bankruptcy.

The Sudden Demise of W.T. Grant.   During the late 1960s and early 1970s, W.T. Grant was one of the country's largest retailers, with sales exceeding $1.6 billion in 1973. From 1966 to 1973, it reported increasing sales each year and a consistent level of profits, as shown in Table 10-1.

Further, investors were apparently pleased with the *consistent* level of profits through 1972, as the stock price remained strong. By 1973, however, investors lost confidence in Grant's reported profits, as the market value dropped by over 75 percent to under $11 per share (see Table 10-2).

With little apparent warning, Grant filed for bankruptcy on October 2, 1975, at which point the New York Stock Exchange suspended trading in its stock. Curiously, the company reported profits and increased sales each year until 1975. However, those

Table 10-1. W.T. Grant
Comparison of Sales and Net Income

	Sales	Net income
	(in millions)	
1966	$ 839	$31
1967	920	31
1968	979	32
1969	1,091	38
1970	1,210	41
1971	1,254	40
1972	1,374	35
1973	1,644	38

Table 10-2. W.T. Grant
Comparison of Stock Price and Net Income

	Closing stock price	Net income (in millions)
1966	$20.750	$31
1967	34.375	31
1968	42.625	32
1969	47.000	38
1970	47.125	41
1971	47.750	40
1972	43.875	35
1973	10.875	38
1974	1.875	8

astute investors and lenders who calculated Grant's CFFO and compared it with its net income would probably have discovered the cash shortage as early as 1969 or 1970—several years before the market at large noted the problem.

As illustrated in Table 10-3, from 1970 through 1974, net income and CFFO provided conflicting signals about Grant's financial health. One important reason for its cash flow problems related to Grant's decentralized system of granting credit. Each store administered its own credit department and had authority either to

Table 10-3. W.T. Grant
Comparison of Net Income and CFFO

	Net income	CFFO
	(in millions)	
1970	$41	$ −1.70
1971	40	−15.30
1972	35	−26.90
1973	38	−114.30
1974	8	−93.20

accept or reject credit applications and to establish credit terms. At most stores, customers were allowed 36 months to pay for their purchases; the minimum monthly payment was $1. With customers purchasing appliances and furniture and paying $1 per month, accounts receivable soared—but cash flows plummeted. Moreover, under accrual accounting methods (in which sales revenue is recorded when the goods are shipped out), profits remained strong even in the face of minimal cash receipts.

Prime Motor Runs out of Gas. Like W.T. Grant, Prime Motor Inns was reporting healthy profits every year—even though the company was having severe cash flow problems. Until its sudden declaration of bankruptcy in September 1990, Prime was one of the country's largest operators of motor inns and hotels. Profits grew 20 percent a year during the 1980s, and its stock price climbed steadily from $1 per share in 1980 to $45 in 1987. By 1990, its revenues topped $400 million, and its market value approached $800 million. Astute investors and lenders studying its cash flows from operations, however, would have noted an ominous trend: CFFO was consistently lower than net income.

Company Profile

Prime Motor Inns

Prime Motor Inns reported strong earnings for 1987–1989, although its CFFO was anemic, an indication of low "quality of earnings."

Prime Motor operated motor inns and hotels (including Howard Johnson, Holiday Inn, Ramada Inn, and Sheraton Inn). In September 1990, the company declared bankruptcy— even though it had reported profits for every quarter as far back as 1986 (with average annual growth over the period of 40 percent). In 1992, Prime's stock was worth $10 million, only a fraction of its valuation in the previous years. See Fig. 10-1.

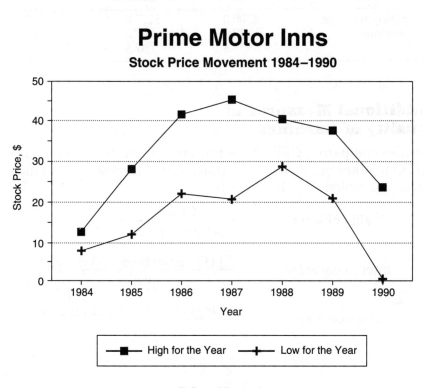

Prime Motor Inns
Stock Price Movement 1984–1990

Prime Motor Inns

Price

Year	High	Low
1984	$13.00	$ 8.08
1985	$28.12	$12.63
1986	$41.25	$22.08
1987	$45.38	$21.00
1988	$40.50	$29.38
1989	$37.50	$21.63
1990	$23.75	$ 0.31

Fig. 10-1.

Consider the operating results for Prime Motor Inns from 1987 to 1989, shown in Table 10-4.

Table 10-4. Prime Motor Inns
Comparison of Operating Revenue, Net Income, and CFFO

	1989	1988	1987
		(in millions)	
Operating revenue	$300.0	$275.0	$225.0
Net income	77.0	67.0	49.0
CFFO	1.8	37.5	7.8

Additional Measures of Quality of Earnings

Besides comparing CFFO to net income, analysts also compare CFFO to other numbers on the statement of income and balance sheet. Examples of such ratios are:

$$\text{Quality of income} = \frac{\text{CFFO}}{\text{operating income}}$$

$$\text{Interest coverage} = \frac{\text{CFFO before taxes and interest}}{\text{interest}}$$

$$\text{Return on assets} = \frac{\text{CFFO before taxes and interest}}{\text{assets}}$$

11

Keep Everything in Balance: Inventory, Sales, and Receivables

While watching the televised special Senate hearings investigating Professor Anita Hill's allegations of sexual harassment against Supreme Court nominee Clarence Thomas, I couldn't help thinking back to the Watergate hearings during the spring of 1973. What began as a bungled burglary of the Democratic National Committee office (located in the Watergate Hotel in Washington) in June 1972 culminated in the unprecedented resignation of a U.S. President in August 1974. The fact that Richard Nixon, who had won reelection by a landslide in 1972, was driven out of office was an affirmation that our system of checks and balances really does work. Both the judicial and the legislative branches played important roles in stopping a chief executive who had abused his constitutional powers. The Supreme Court ruled unanimously that President Nixon's firing of special prosecutor Archibald Cox, who was leading the investigation, was unconstitutional; and the House of Representatives's Judiciary Committee recommended impeachment to the full House, making it probable that Nixon would have been impeached and convicted by the Senate.

Whether the goal is preserving a democracy or upholding the integrity of financial reporting, a system of checks and balances is paramount for preventing, uncovering, and punishing financial improprieties. And much like the U.S. government, financial reporting has three separate "branches": a statement of income, a statement of cash flows, and a balance sheet. When one of these financial reports contains shenanigans, warning signs generally appear in the other statements. The previous chapter demonstrated how cash flow analysis might be used to detect shenanigans on the statement of income. This chapter shows how the balance sheet might be used to uncover shenanigans on the statement of income and to assess the quality of earnings.

Checklist: Signs of Misleading Financial Statements That May Appear on the Balance Sheet

1. Overstating assets or showing balances at amounts in excess of their net realizable values

2. Understating assets—where companies attempt to "smooth" income by shifting future expenses into the current fiscal year

3. Understating liabilities, either by excluding them entirely from the balance sheet or by recording overly conservative estimates of future obligations

4. Overstating liabilities—using reserves to smooth income by shifting current-year revenue to the future

5. Misstating owners' equity

Relationships between the Balance Sheet and the Income Statement

Watch the Amount of Capital

To understand the purpose of the balance sheet and the statement of income, consider the following analogy. Think of a balance sheet as a partly filled bathtub, and any water added or removed during the period covered by the balance sheet as the income or loss for that period. The amount of water in the tub at any point in time can be compared to the amount of capital (or owners' equity) on the balance sheet. If too much water is added to the tub or not enough water is removed, the water level will be too high. Similarly, if too much revenue is recorded or not enough expenses are written off against income, the capital will be too high.

An investigator attempting to determine whether too much water was added (or not enough removed) might study the water level in the tub. If the level recently rose far higher than its normal level, he or she would conclude that the flow of water into the tub during the period was higher than normal or that the outflow was abnormally low. Similarly, an analyst attempting to determine whether too much revenue was recognized (or too few expenses charged) might study a company's level of capital and its assets on the balance sheet. If the capital or assets grew faster than expected (in relationship to the growth in sales), the analyst might become concerned that earnings were slowing or that the company's assets were bloated.

Overstated Assets Can Signal Problems to Come

A reliable early warning sign of shenanigans on the statement of income is the presence of overstated assets on the balance sheet. In particular, overstated inventory or accounts receivable often portend sudden future declines in earnings. (As shown in the appendix to this chapter, financial ratios that measure the growth in assets over time and their relationship to growth in sales can indicate whether assets are overstated.)

The Relationship between Sales and Inventory

Think of inventory as merchandise waiting to be sold. A company tries to anticipate future sales and stocks inventory to meet that demand. In most cases, growth in inventory should mirror growth in sales. One sign of trouble is when inventory is growing much faster than sales, possibly indicating that inventory is not selling well or is obsolete. Consider how the bloated inventory on one company's balance sheet signaled a future downturn in profits.

Crazy Eddie. A fast-growing company with out-of-control inventory was New York City-based electronic equipment retailer Crazy Eddie. An early warning that Crazy Eddie was having problems was that inventory was growing much more rapidly than sales. As Table 11-1 shows, from 1985 to 1986, sales increased 88 percent, but inventory jumped 125 percent. This problem persisted in 1987 when sales increased 34 percent, but inventory increased 83 percent.

Table 11-1. Crazy Eddie
Changes in Sales and Inventory

	2/28/87		2/28/86		2/28/85
			(in millions)		
Sales	$352.5		$262.3		$139.3
Increase:		+34.4%		+88.3%	
Inventory	$109.1		$ 59.6		$ 26.5
Increase:		+83.1%		+124.9%	

Company Profile

Crazy Eddie

Crazy Eddie was charged with issuing fraudulent financial statements by overstating its inventory.

In 1970, Eddie Antar and his dad Sam opened Crazy Eddie in Brooklyn, New York. With discount pricing and aggressive selling, the business took off. Business expanded rapidly, and at its height in 1987, Crazy Eddie operated 43 stores with annual sales of $350 million and a stock market valuation of $600 million.

In September 1984, Crazy Eddie went public at a split-adjusted price of $2 per share; five months later the share price reached $20. Investors at first reaped huge rewards, as many of their shares rose more than 10 times in value in 20 months. See Fig. 11-1.

Crazy Eddie
Stock Price Movement 1984–1989

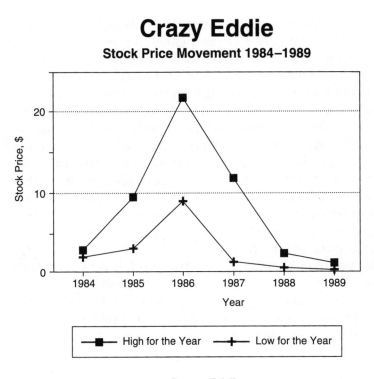

Crazy Eddie

Price

Year	High	Low
1984	$ 2.88	$2.00
1985	$ 9.63	$2.88
1986	$21.63	$9.13
1987	$11.63	$1.25
1988	$ 2.25	$0.50
1989	$ 0.94	$0.19

Fig. 11-1.

Crazy Eddie's Inventory Was Going Crazy. Although the company appeared to be healthy, its inventory management was out of control. It tracked inventory manually, mostly by an antiquated system of blue file cards in each store. The company's mushrooming inventory demands eventually overwhelmed the warehouse staff.

Word began spreading that Crazy Eddie was fiddling with its inventory and profit reports to maintain its high stock price.

According to the allegations in several lawsuits against the company, Crazy Eddie falsely recorded sales to other chains (i.e., wholesale transactions) as if they were retail sales. For instance, it would sell 100 TVs with a retail value of $40,000 to another chain for $20,000—but would still record a profit of $20,000.

Other allegations of inventory shenanigans included: (1) inclusion within inventory of damaged merchandise sent back to the manufacturer, and (2) fabricated debit memos (which reduced the amount owed by the company to suppliers) to understate the company's debt. Moreover, the court papers alleged under-the-table deals in which Eddie and his family sold between $5 million and $10 million worth of merchandise without ever recording a transaction, and then pocketed the profits themselves.

And Eddie Went Off the Deep End.   The end came quickly for Eddie. On December 22, 1986, Eddie Antar resigned as president; and in January 1987, he gave up his title as chief executive officer. Chilling financial news followed shortly thereafter. In January, the company reported that same-store sales for the prior quarter had dropped 20 percent and that net income had plunged 90 percent.

The Relationship between
Sales and Accounts Receivable

Whenever a company sells merchandise on account, it ships merchandise before it is paid for. In most cases, inventory growth should mirror growth in sales. That is, if sales are growing by 10 percent, accounts receivable should also be growing by about 10 percent. If accounts receivable are growing much faster than sales, it usually means that the company is having trouble collecting from customers. If the condition persists, the company will eventually experience negative cash flows. Consider how the inflated accounts receivable on Equatorial Communications' balance sheet provided an excellent clue that the company was heading for trouble.

Equatorial Communications.   In 1984, Equatorial Communications posted revenue of $38.3 million, up 114 percent over the previous year. Unfortunately, though, accounts receivable was growing even faster—a sign that the company was having difficulty collecting from its customers. As Table 11-2 shows, from

Table 11-2. Equatorial Communications
Changes in Sales and Receivables

	12/31/84		12/31/83		12/31/82
			(in millions)		
Sales	$38.3		$17.9		$9.6
Increase:		+114.0%		+86.4%	
Receivables	$10.2		$ 2.7		$1.3
Increase:		+277.8%		+107.7%	

1982 to 1983, sales increased 86 percent, yet receivables jumped 108 percent. The following year, sales increased 114 percent, yet receivables were up 278 percent.

Company Profile

Equatorial Communications

Equatorial Communications was having difficulty collecting from customers, as receivables were growing much faster than sales.

Equatorial was a fast-growing player in the satellite telecommunications business during the early 1980s. From 1982 through 1984, its annual sales grew at better than 100 percent, with equally impressive growth in earnings. Equatorial's stock peaked at $22.25 per share in 1984 before beginning a swift and permanent decline. See Fig. 11-2.

Sales versus Both Inventory and Accounts Receivable

As demonstrated earlier, a company is likely to face problems if either inventory or receivables is growing much faster than sales. If both categories are growing faster than sales, the problems are magnified. Consider how bloated inventory and accounts receivable both served as early warning signs of a collapse in earnings and cash flows for Regina Company.

Regina Company.   For years, Regina was a major seller of vacuum cleaners. As shown in Table 11-3, its sales and profits grew steadily from 1985 to 1988.

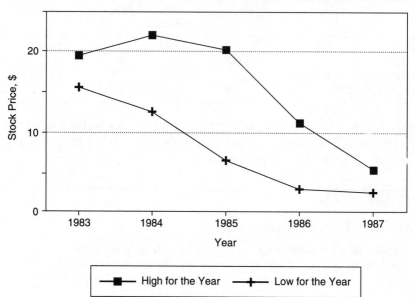

Equatorial Communications
Stock Price Movement 1983–1987

Equatorial Communications

	Price	
Year	High	Low
1983	$19.50	$15.50
1984	$22.25	$12.63
1985	$20.25	$ 6.38
1986	$11.13	$ 2.63
1987	$ 5.13	$ 2.38

Fig. 11-2.

Table 11-3. Regina Company
Changes in Sales and Net Income

	Sales	Net income
	(in millions)	
1985	$ 67.7	$ 1.1
1986	76.1	4.1
1987	128.2	7.1
1988	181.1	10.9

Table 11-4. Regina Company
Stock Price

	High	Low
1985	$ 6.50	$ 5.38
1986	10.88	5.78
1987	22.38	10.00
1988	27.50	3.75

Further, Regina's stock performed well—until the bottom fell out in 1988; see Table 11-4.

Company Profile

Regina Company

Regina Company reported record profits in 1988, but investors and lenders should have been wary, because both receivables and inventory had grown much faster than sales.

As recently as 1988, Regina was a leading seller of vacuum cleaners and floor-care products. Its sales had increased at an annual rate of 119 percent over the two previous years, setting records for both sales and earnings. Regina's market value approached $250 million in 1988. See Fig. 11-3.

In September 1988, Regina's CEO announced that its annual report for June 30, 1988, contained materially incorrect financial information and would have to be restated. Several days later, he abruptly resigned. The stock price, which reached $27.50 in August, closed at $4 at the end of September on volume 21 times greater than that of the prior month. By comparing the increases in sales with the changes in both receivables and inventory during the period immediately preceding the surprise announcement, investors and lenders would have been duly warned.

Table 11-5 shows that, for the quarter ended March 31, 1988, Regina's sales grew a healthy 28 percent, but its inventory increased 52 percent, and receivables increased 54 percent—a sign that inventory was not selling and that receivables were not being collected. More extreme were the results for the year ended June

Regina Company

Stock Price Movement 1985–1989

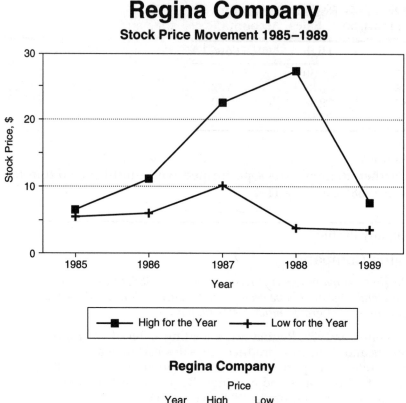

Regina Company

	Price	
Year	High	Low
1985	$ 6.43	$ 5.38
1986	$10.88	$ 5.80
1987	$22.38	$10.00
1988	$27.50	$ 3.75
1989	$ 7.38	$ 3.38

Fig. 11-3.

30, 1988. Sales were up 41 percent, but inventory jumped 100 percent, and receivables ballooned 187 percent.

With both inventory and receivables increasing much more rapidly than sales, shrewd analysts and investors should have detected a major warning sign when the March 31 financial statements were released. Unfortunately for those who failed to notice this warning, the stock price fell almost 85 percent from August to September.

Table 11-5. Regina Company
Comparison of Sales, Accounts Receivable, and Inventory

	Quarter ended		Year ended	
	3/31/88	3/31/87	6/30/88	6/30/87
		(in millions)		
Sales	$47.0	$36.7	$181.1	$128.2
Increase		*+28.0%*		*+41.0%*
Inventory	$45.7	$30.0	$ 39.1	$ 19.6
Increase		*+52.3%*		*+100.0%*
Receivables	$42.8	$27.8	$ 51.1	$ 17.8
Increase		*+54.0%*		*+187.1%*

Appendix. Other Early Warning Signs on the Balance Sheet

Uncollectibility of Receivables

Warning Signs

Large amount of overdue receivables

Large increase in receivables with flat sales

Exaggerated dependence on one or two customers

Related-party receivables

Slow receivables turnover

Receivables consisting largely of goods that customers may return

Inadequate Salability of Inventory

Warning Signs

Slow inventory turnover

Large increase when sales are flat

Faddish inventory

Collateralized inventory

Insufficient insurance

Change of corporate inventory valuation methods

Increase in the number of LIFO pools

Inclusion of inflation profits in inventory

Large, unexplained increase in inventory

Inclusion of improper costs in inventory

Improper Valuation of Investments
Warning Signs

Switching between current and noncurrent categories

Investments recorded in excess of costs

Risky investments that must be written off

Obsolescence of Fixed Assets
Warning Signs

Old equipment and technology

High maintenance and repair expense

Declining output level

Inadequate depreciation charge

Change in depreciation method

Lengthening depreciation period

Decline in depreciation expense

Large write-off of assets

Overstatement of Intangibles
Warning Signs

Slow amortization period

Lengthening amortization period

High ratio of intangibles to total assets and capital

Large balance in goodwill even though profits are weak

Checklist: Warnings That May Appear on the Balance Sheet

Where to look	Concern	Warning Signs
		Assets
Cash	Restricted	A portion is restricted
Receivables	Collection	Large overdue receivables Large increase with sales flat Overly dependent on one or two customers Related-party receivables Slow receivables turnover Right of return exists
Inventory	Salability	Slow inventory turnover Large increase when sales are flat Collateralized inventory Insufficient insurance Changing methods Increasing LIFO pools Large increase in inventory Improper costs included
Investments	Realization	Switching between current and noncurrent categories Investments recorded in excess of costs Risky investments that must be written off
Fixed Assets	Obsolescent	Old equipment and technology High maintenance expense Declining output level Inadequate depreciation charge Change in depreciation method Lengthening of depreciation period Decline in depreciation Large write-off of assets

Where to look	Concern	Warning Signs
	Assets	
Intangibles	Overstated	Slow amortization period
		Lengthening of amortization period
		High ratio of intangibles to total assets and owners' equity
		Large balance in goodwill although profits are weak
	Liabilities	
Estimated liabilities	Understated	Amortize warranties quickly
		Arbitrary adjustments
	Smoothing	Over-reserve warranties

12

Preventing
Shenanigans

How Can Shenanigans Be Prevented?

Because of the potentially dire consequences for investors and lenders who rely on misleading financial statements, actions must be undertaken to prevent shenanigans. Shenanigan prevention should involve a four-pronged attack, aimed at:

1. *Improving auditors' ability to audit.* Since investors and lenders rely heavily on the auditor catching any accounting tricks, auditor training should place greater emphasis on this skill.

2. *Improving training for users of financial reports.* Investors and lenders, who rely heavily on representations in financial reports, must be trained to search for accounting tricks.

3. *Improving the control environment within organizations.* Financial improprieties are less likely to occur in organizations with strong financial controls. Such controls include internal auditors, independent auditors, an audit committee, and independent members on the board of directors. Moreover, regulatory oversight by the SEC serves as an additional control.

4. *Restructuring managers' incentives.* Management incentives that reward honest financial reporting and punish the kinds of

shenanigans described in this book would reduce the likeli-
hood of managers using such trickery. An ethical tone must be
established at the top of the organization.

Some Encouraging Signs—The Treadway Commission

A milestone in shenanigan-prevention history was reached in 1985
with the formation of the National Commission on Fraudulent
Financial Reporting, chaired by former SEC Commissioner James
C. Treadway, Jr. The Treadway Commission undertook a compre-
hensive study of the financial reporting system in the United States
in response to a request that it "identify causal factors that can lead
to fraudulent financial reporting and steps to reduce its incidence."

The commission was a private-sector initiative, jointly spon-
sored and funded by the American Institute of Certified Public
Accountants (AICPA), the American Accounting Association
(AAA), the Financial Executives Institute (FEI), the Institute of
Internal Auditors (IIA), and the National Association of
Accountants (NAA), now called the Institute of Management
Accountants (IMA).

Its Conclusions and Recommendations

In October 1987, the Treadway Commission published a series of
recommendations addressed specifically to: (1) the top management and board of directors of all public companies, (2) independent public accountants and the public accounting profession, (3)
the SEC and other regulatory and law enforcement bodies, and
(4) the academic community. Here is a summary of some of its
most important recommendations.

For the Company and Its Top Management and Directors

- Set the proper tone at the top, demonstrating an understanding
  of the factors that may cause the financial statements to be
  fraudulently misstated.

- Maintain internal controls that are adequate to prevent and detect fraudulent reporting.

- Develop and enforce written codes of corporate conduct. This should foster a strong ethical climate and open channels of communication to help protect against fraudulent reporting. Additionally, the audit committee of the board should review compliance with the code annually, including compliance by top management.

- Companies should maintain an effective internal audit function staffed with adequate personnel. Besides reviewing the financial aspects of the company, the internal auditors should consider the implications of their nonfinancial audit findings for the financial reporting function. The internal auditors should work with and report directly to the audit committee of the board to ensure their independence.

- Audit committees should take an active role in reviewing and evaluating management and should serve as an independent link to the external auditor.

- Management should communicate directly to stockholders in the annual report about the company's financial statements and its internal controls. Managers should discuss their responsibilities for the controls and the integrity of the financial reports and should assess the company's internal controls.

- When a public company changes outside accountants, it should disclose to the SEC the nature of any material accounting or auditing issues discussed with its old and new auditors during the three-year period preceding the change.

- The audit committee should increase its oversight for quarterly financial reports, approving these reports before public release.

For the Independent Public Accountant

- Auditors should have more responsibility for the detection of fraudulent financial reporting during an audit.

- Auditors should be required to review quarterly financial statements before the statements are released to the public.

- Accounting firms should recognize and control the organizational and individual pressures that potentially reduce audit quality.

For the SEC and Other Regulators

- The SEC should have the authority to impose fines in administrative proceedings and to seek fines from a court directly in injunctive proceedings.
- The SEC should have the authority to issue cease-and-desist orders when a securities law violation or an unsound financial reporting practice is found. (The SEC now has such authority.)
- The SEC should seek explicit statutory authority to bar or suspend corporate officers and directors involved in fraudulent financial reporting from future service in that capacity.
- Criminal prosecution of fraudulent financial reporting cases should be made a higher priority.

For the Academic Community

- Throughout the business and accounting curricula, educators should foster knowledge and understanding of the factors that may cause fraudulent financial reporting and the strategies that can reduce its incidence.
- The business and accounting curricula should promote a better understanding of the function and importance of internal controls, including the control environment, in preventing, detecting, and deterring fraudulent financial reporting.
- The curricula should emphasize ethical values by integrating their development with the acquisition of knowledge and skills to help prevent, detect, and deter fraudulent financial reporting.
- The CPA examination should test students on the ethical values that further the understanding of fraudulent financial reporting and the information skills that promote its reduction.
- As part of their continuing education, independent public accountants, internal auditors, and corporate accountants should study the forces and opportunities that contribute to fraudulent financial reporting and the risk factors that may indicate their occurrence.

After Treadway

The reaction to the Treadway Commission report has been largely favorable throughout the business community. In fact, various accounting organizations, including the Institute of Management Accountants and the American Institute of Certified Public Accountants, have prepared videotapes to make their members more aware of fraudulent financial reporting issues. Universities and regulators have also been busy integrating the Treadway recommendations into their training programs.

The real measure of the commission's success in reducing fraudulent financial reporting, however, will ultimately lie in the actual reduction of fraudulent financial reports. On that score, as such recent fiascos as College Bound and Maxwell Communications illustrate, the recommendations in Treadway's report may have thus far failed to reach those companies that need them most.

While we all yearn for a shenanigan-free world, until it arrives, readers of financial statements should be actively searching for misleading information in financial reports. The following checklists will be helpful in this pursuit.

Checklist 1: Signs of Misleading Financial Statements

Management decision	Investor's concern
Choosing accounting policies	Too liberal
Changing accounting policies	Unjustified
Deferring expenses	Profits are overstated
Income smoothing	Profits are understated
Recognizing revenue too soon	Profits are overstated
Expense is underaccrued	Profits are overstated
	Liabilities are understated
Expense is overaccrued	Profits are understated
Taking a "big bath"	Future profits are boosted
Changing discretionary cost	Manipulating profits
Low quality controls	Risk of shenanigans
Change in auditor	Risk of shenanigans

Checklist 2: 52 Techniques for Finding Shenanigans

1. Be alert for misguided management incentives.
2. Watch for poor internal accounting controls.
3. Question overly liberal accounting rules.
4. Watch for qualified opinions.
5. Favor companies with conservative accounting policies.
6. Be alert for aggressive inventory valuation.
7. Consider the significance of pending or imminent litigation.
8. Question long-term purchase commitments.
9. Watch for changes in accounting principles.
10. Read the letter from the president with a grain of salt.
11. Focus on management and its estimates.
12. Be wary when the auditor and/or lawyer resign abruptly.
13. Watch for early shipping, before sale occurs.
14. Weigh uncertainties of companies' using the percentage-of-completion method.
15. Look for improper use of the percentage-of-completion method.
16. Check whether the risks and the benefits have transferred to the buyer.
17. Determine whether the buyer is likely to return the goods.
18. Check if the buyer has financing to pay.
19. Determine whether the customer is obligated to pay.
20. Watch for hasty recognition of franchise revenue.
21. Question how retailers account for returned goods.
22. Be alert for revenue recorded on the exchange of property.
23. Determine whether management estimates are realistic.
24. Watch for the sale of pooled assets acquired in a business combination.
25. Be alert for tricks with LIFO pools.
26. Watch for gains from the sale of undervalued investments, including real estate.
27. Don't be fooled by "profits" from retiring debt.
28. Adjust for the mixing of gains from recurring and nonrecurring activities.

29. Watch for co-mingling operating/nonoperating income.
30. Be alert for companies hiding losses as "noncontinuing."
31. Watch for the capitalization of start-up costs.
32. Consider the propriety of capitalizing R&D costs.
33. Look for companies that capitalize advertising.
34. Watch for companies that capitalize administrative costs.
35. Question companies that depreciate fixed assets too slowly.
36. Be alert for lengthy amortization periods.
37. Be concerned when the depreciation or amortization period increases.
38. Watch for bad loans and other uncollectibles that have not been written off.
39. Be wary of worthless investments.
40. Ascertain that cash received has been earned.
41. Probe for a troubled company with fixed payments.
42. Watch for an unrecorded postretirement liability.
43. Read debt covenants carefully for contingencies.
44. Examine any debt for equity swaps.
45. Be wary of companies using subsidiaries for borrowing.
46. Watch for defeasance of debt.
47. Be critical of successful companies with large reserves.
48. Be alert for prepayment of operating expenses.
49. Be concerned when the depreciation or amortization period decreases.
50. Use cash flow analysis to measure quality of earnings.
51. Compare growth in sales with growth in inventory.
52. Compare growth in sales with growth in receivables.

The Goal of Financial Reporting

The primary goal in financial reporting is the dissemination of financial statements that accurately measure the profitability and financial condition of a company. To ascertain that those financial reports are accurate, investors and lenders focus on the following seven guiding principles.

*Guiding principle 1: Revenue should be recorded after
the earnings process has been completed and an
exchange has occurred. Similarly, a gain should be
recorded when a nonoperating asset is sold at above
its book value.*

For most businesses, the appropriate time to record revenue
from selling a product or providing a service is when two conditions have been met: (1) The earnings process is substantially
complete, and (2) there has been an arm's-length exchange.
Additionally, the risks and benefits of ownership of the product
must have transferred from the seller to the buyer in order for a
sale to be recognized.

Consider the accounting for the sale of a new McDonald's franchise. McDonald's receives a large initial payment for the various
kinds of assistance it will provide the franchisee over the years.
Since much of the money it receives is still "unearned," McDonald's
should record only a part of the initial payment as revenue.

Increase:	Cash	1,000	
Increase:	Revenue		250
Increase:	. Unearned Revenue		750

When to Capital Assets

*Guiding principle 2: An enterprise should capitalize
costs incurred that produce a future benefit and
expense those that produce no such benefit.*

Assets represent economic resources of the enterprise which
are expected to provide some future benefit for the enterprise.
Assets are initially recorded at their historic cost. However, if the
anticipated future benefits dissipate, either gradually or suddenly, the asset account must be reduced to reflect the lower-than-
expected economic benefit.

One area that may create some controversy and disagreements
between management and the independent auditor is knowing
whether there is indeed a future benefit. This issue may arise in
the following situations:

1. Initially, when a company incurs a cost (e.g., in purchasing
   equipment or office supplies).

2. If the initial decision had been to record as an asset (i.e., to "capitalize" it), a decision must then be made over how long a period the benefit will be derived and in what proportion each year.
3. If there is a sudden and permanent decline in the value of the asset, when and how much of the asset should be written off as a loss.

If the amount of the asset is insignificant ("immaterial"), or if the benefit will be received over a short time horizon, then the cost should be reflected immediately as an expense rather than as an asset.

Guiding principle 3: As an enterprise realizes the benefit from using an asset, the asset or a part thereof should be written off as an expense of the period.

As an enterprise realizes the benefit from using an asset, the expired portion of the asset must be transferred to an expense account, and, of course, the asset account must be decreased by a similar amount. This is a common and natural process. A company acquires resources to produce benefits—generating additional revenue and profits. Over time those resources are used in the productive process, and revenue and profits are realized. At that point, a portion of the assets should be transferred to the appropriate expense accounts. For example, inventory is classified as an asset when the raw material is first acquired. When the product is completed and sold, however, the entire cost of the product would be transferred from the inventory account (an asset) to cost of goods sold (the corresponding expense).

Increase:	Cost of Goods Sold	500	
Decrease:	Merchandise Inventory		500

Guiding principle 4: When there is a sudden and substantial impairment in an asset's value, the asset should be written off immediately and in its entirety, rather than gradually over time.

Since assets represent future benefits of an enterprise, in the event that the benefit no longer exists, the asset should be written off *as a loss* as soon as it becomes determinable. The term "big bath" is used to describe large write-offs of assets whose value suddenly declines and must be written off.

Thus, when a company closes a plant, it should make an accounting entry that records a loss and eliminates the asset account, Plant and Equipment.

Increase:	Loss on Plant Closing	1,000,000	
Decrease:	Plant and Equipment		1,000,000

Guiding principle 5: An enterprise has incurred a liability if it is obligated to make future sacrifices.

A liability represents a present obligation of an enterprise to perform some act or to sacrifice some resource in the future. A common shenanigan is an attempt to hide or "keep off the books" actual or probable liabilities. This technique is referred to as "off-balance-sheet financing."

Going back to our McDonald's franchise, the portion of the initial payment to McDonald's that was unearned should be recorded as a liability [since future services (sacrifices) are required].

Guiding principle 6: Revenue should be recorded in the period in which it is earned.

Under the accrual basis of accounting, revenue should be recorded in the period in which it is earned rather than in the period in which cash is received.

Guiding principle 7: Expenses should be charged against income in the period in which the benefit is received.

Generally accepted accounting principles require that expenses should be "matched" with revenue. Thus expenses must be charged in the period in which the enterprise realizes a benefit from using assets to produce or sell its product.

13

A Century of Shenanigans

That which hath been is that which will be,
And that which hath been done is that
which shall be done;
And there is nothing new under the sun.
KING SOLOMON
Ecclesiastes

As it was for Solomon, so it still is with "get rich quick" schemes and financial shenanigans.

Pre-World War II Scams

The first half of this century witnessed numerous instances of financial shenanigans in corporate annual reports, leading to grossly overvalued stock prices and contributing to the collapse of the stock market between 1929 and 1932. For example, the price of International Power, Inc.'s stock dropped 78 points in a single day when it was reported that the company had "cooked its books."

In addition to issuing misleading corporate financial reports, swindlers and con artists (such as Charles Ponzi, Ivar Kreuger, and Philip Musica) caused investors and bondholders to suffer great losses. One such scam occurred just after World War I, when many unsuspecting souls were reportedly swindled out of nearly $400 million in fraudulent liberty bonds.

A decade later, infamous Charles ("Get Rich Quick") Ponzi, perhaps the best-known con artist in history, duped investors with promises of incredibly high returns. Ponzi, of course, used the money of late-coming investors to pay high returns to early investors—a technique known ever since as a Ponzi scheme. Ponzi reportedly raised at least $15 million before *The Boston Globe* exposed his scheme. He was later sentenced to 10 years in prison for larceny and mail fraud.

A later and far larger financial scam was perpetrated by international financier Ivar Kreuger. He often switched companies' assets and liabilities or created fictitious assets when existing ones weren't enough. After an extensive investigation, authorities found that Kreuger had bilked shareholders and moneylenders out of $500 million.

The late 1920s and 1930s witnessed the rise and fall of Philip Musica, alias Frank Donald Coster. A fugitive who was a convicted and twice-jailed swindler, Musica used fraudulent means and profits from the illegal sale of alcohol to purchase the McKesson & Robbins drug company, which subsequently named him its president. For years thereafter, he successfully hoodwinked banks, embezzled millions of dollars from the company, and fraudulently misrepresented its financial reports. One way he misrepresented those reports was by listing nonexistent inventory (generally accepted auditing standards at that time did not require that inventory taking be observed). The auditors eventually caught on to the scheme in 1937, when they discovered that $10 million of inventory and $9 million of accounts receivable at McKesson & Robbins were fictitious (out of assets of $87 million). Musica shot himself on December 16, 1938.

More Recent Shenanigans

During the second half of this century, the size and frequency of financial chicanery increased dramatically. Among the more notable scams during the 1960s, 1970s, and 1980s were the Great Salad Oil Swindle, Equity Funding Corporation, Wedtech Corporation, and Lincoln Savings & Loan (part of the savings & loan debacle of the 1980s).

The Great Salad Oil Swindle

In 1963 it was reported that Anthony (Tino) De Angelis of Allied Crude Vegetable Oil Refining Corporation had devised an ingenious way of overstating the company's inventory of salad oil: He filled many of its vats with water, adding only a top layer of oil. Pipes connected the vats underground, so that the layer of oil could be shifted across the vats as needed during the inventory observation procedure.

For the better part of a decade, financiers loaned hundreds of millions of dollars to De Angelis to bankroll his worldwide salad oil deals. He had a vast storage center for salad oil in Bayonne, New Jersey, and each time he got a loan, he pledged part of his salad oil stock as collateral. He didn't ship the salad oil to the financiers, but merely gave them papers stating that the oil was their property until the loan was repaid.

Finally, in November 1963, De Angelis's salad oil company collapsed when the auditors discovered that the salad oil tanks were almost empty. De Angelis had sold his financiers $175 million of phantom salad oil—and the money was gone.

Equity Funding Corporation—
Wall Street's Watergate

One of the most massive and sensational financial frauds perpetrated by a major company occurred at Equity Funding Corporation of America during the 1960s and 1970s. (In fact, the story was subsequently made into a movie.) Equity Funding, a financial services institution, began operations in 1960 with $10,000. By 1973, the company purported to manage assets of $1 billion. Its record growth during the previous decade had exceeded that of all major diversified financial companies in the United States.

In April 1973, this "growth" was exposed as a fiction. After adjustments, the year-end 1972 reported net worth of $143.4 million was restated to a *negative* $42.1 million. Equity Funding's stock, which had traded as high as $80 a share, became worthless; and the company filed for bankruptcy. Shockingly, according to court records, the company had engaged in "fictitious entries in certain receivable and income accounts" *as early as 1965.* Out of 99,000 policies representing $3.5 billion in insurance on the books, 56,000 policies representing $2 billion were fictitious. Equity Funding had faked assets of more than $100 million; it had counterfeited bonds—and forged death certificates.

In November 1973, 22 people—20 of them former employees of Equity Funding, the other two its auditors—were indicted on 105 counts of fraud and conspiracy. Stanley Goldblum, the company's co-founder and former president, was sentenced to eight years in federal prison for his part in the fraud.

Welbilt Electronic Die Corporation—Wedtech

The 1980s were a period of rapidly rising stock prices, fueled in part by governmental deregulation—coupled with outrageous financial shenanigans. One of the most widely reported cases of financial improprieties occurred at Wedtech Corporation in the South Bronx in New York City.

Wedtech, a machine shop, was founded in 1965. Using a variety of fraudulent means, including bribing government officials, lying on government proposals and contracts, and misrepresenting its financial performance, the company caused investors to lose tens of millions of dollars in worthless stock.

One vehicle for its fraudulent financial reports was the inappropriate use of the percentage-of-completion method for recording revenue. (See Chapter 5 for more on this shenanigan.) Wedtech improperly accelerated its contract receipts, falsified invoices, reported revenue on contracts never received, paid bribes to government officials, and claimed falsely that the company was controlled by a Hispanic (thereby qualifying the company for favored status in receiving government contracts).

Besides charges of bribery and fraud against Wedtech officials, lawsuits seeking $105 million in damages have been filed against the company's auditors, charging that they knew about the fraud, corporate waste, and inaccurate financial reporting.

Lincoln Savings & Loan

While all the previous financial frauds are noteworthy and trouble-some, based on sheer size and the number of people affected, nothing compares to the financial shenanigans committed in the savings & loan industry during the 1980s. Estimates of the cost to taxpayers to bail out the industry run as high as $500 billion—or $2,000 for every man, woman, and child in the United States. That sum is greater than the combined inflation-adjusted cost of the Marshall Plan (which rebuilt Europe after World War II) and the bailouts of Chrysler Corporation, Continental Bank, and New York City.

While numerous S&Ls were guilty of poor judgment, questionable business practices, and creative accounting, many (including American Diversified of Costa Mesa, California, and Vernon Savings of Vernon, Texas) perpetuated massive frauds. No S&L failure, however, has stirred more interest and outrage than that of Lincoln Savings & Loan, which not only is expected to cost American taxpayers a record $2.5 billion but also allegedly involved the use of members of Congress (i.e., the "Keating Five") to influence banking regulators.

Charles Keating, who ran Lincoln Savings, used government-insured deposits to speculate on a massive and perhaps unprece-dented scale. For example, he wagered $100 million of such deposits in a risk-arbitrage fund owned and operated by convicted shenanigan grandmaster Ivan Boesky. He also bought bonds from Eastern Airlines at a little more than par shortly before Eastern filed for bankruptcy. In fact, in its 1988 examination of Lincoln, the FDIC found that 77 percent of its bonds were "junk bonds."

Moreover, Lincoln's parent, American Continental Corpora-tion (ACC), gave new meaning to the term nepotism, by includ-ing among its top eight officers not only Keating but also his son, daughter, and son-in-law. Some held top positions, receiving half a million dollars or more in salary, at ages 24 to 28 (with his son pulling down a cool $900,000). In fact, from 1985 to 1988, Keating and members of his family took out $34 million in salary and sales of ACC stock.

After ACC filed for bankruptcy in April 1989, federal investigators hired Kenneth Leventhal & Co., a leading real estate accounting firm, to examine Lincoln's real estate investments and loans. For every one of the 15 deals that it reviewed, Leventhal concluded that a profit should never have been recorded. In each deal, Leventhal said, Lincoln entered into some form of related transaction that had the effect of either nullifying the deal or making its contribution to Lincoln's income far less than reported.

Later that same month, the federal government seized control of Lincoln, claiming that it was being operated in an unsafe and unsound manner. Keating and his family were accused of looting the bank of $1.1 billion. Most of the family is being sued by 23,000 people who say they were conned out of $250 million worth of uninsured bonds.

Curiously, Keating refused to be an officer or a director of Lincoln. When asked why by a representative of the Federal Home Loan Bank of Seattle, he reportedly said that he "did not want to go to jail." (Unfortunately for him, a judge still sentenced him in April 1992 to a 10-year term.)

Shenanigans during the 1990s

During the 1990s, the pace of accounting scams has continued unabated. Some of these (such as BCCI and Maxwell Communications) have had global repercussions, while others have rocked and embarrassed local communities (such as College Bound of Boca Raton, Florida).

Bank of Commerce and Credit International (BCCI)

When it was founded almost 20 years ago, BCCI was proclaimed as the Bank of the Third World, extending services to Arab oil sheiks and hard-working Muslim immigrants in Europe. But eventually BCCI's arms-open approach attracted drug smugglers and embezzling dictators, who used the bank to launder millions in illegal profits. By the late 1980s and early 1990s, it had become the bank of choice for the underworld and such nefarious characters as terrorist Abu Nidal and dictator Manuel Noriega.

In July 1991, regulators from eight countries shut down BCCI (now often referred to as the Bank of Crooks and Criminals, International). In the 1991 indictment, New York District Attorney Robert Morganthau described BCCI as "the largest bank fraud in world financial history." An estimated *$20 billion* was stolen, lost, or swindled.

Maxwell Communications

Although it was no match for BCCI in sheer size, the massive fraud allegedly perpetrated by billionaire Robert Maxwell, head of Maxwell Communications, was equally "daring." The story began unraveling shortly after Robert Maxwell's body was found floating off the Canary Islands on November 5, 1991. In the days and weeks that followed, investigators found that he had engaged in a massive fraud to stave off the imminent collapse of his corporate empire, which included the publishing giant Macmillan, Inc., and such newspapers as the *New York Daily News* and the London-based *Daily Mirror.*

Overwhelmed by debt, Maxwell allegedly resorted to one of history's great financial frauds, looting over $1.4 billion from Maxwell Communications, including $800 million from the employees' pension plan. Investigators also found some accounting gimmicks used by Mr. Maxwell, such as artificially inflating earnings through bogus real estate sales to other firms under his control. (See Chapter 6 for more on this shenanigan.)

Considerably smaller scams, but much closer to home, have rocked and riveted the south Florida resort community of Boca Raton. Because of the number of scams in that area, some financial writers have dubbed this beautiful strip along the Atlantic Ocean "maggot's mile."

College Bound, Inc.

College Bound, a college test preparation company, went public in late 1988 by merging into an existing "shell" corporation. A penny stock until early 1990, its stock price reached $24 per share (worth one-quarter of $1 billion) in August 1991, growing by more than 800 percent in just one year. Moreover, its sales jumped from under $3 million in 1989 to $20 million by 1991. Such rapid growth aroused interest not only among investors, but also among financial writers. The earliest questions were raised by *Barron's* in May 1991, when it challenged some of College Bound's aggressive accounting policies of capitalizing, rather than expensing, costs associated with opening new testing centers. A second national publication raised troubling questions in December 1991, when *USA Today* columnist Dan Dorfman reported that College Bound's real growth, as measured by operating revenues, may have been overstated. With these and other allegations about the integrity of its financial reports, I decided to use the techniques described in this book to evaluate independently whether College Bound had used financial shenanigans to dress up its financial reports. My conclusions, first reported in an article entitled "College Bound: Fortune 500 Bound or Fantasy Bound?" (published by Dow Jones News Retrieval on January 9, 1992), are summarized below.

Findings.   Among the major concerns raised in my article on College Bound were the following:

1. Apparently inadequate background and experience of the independent auditor
2. Questionable accounting policies relating to quality of earnings
3. Circumventing SEC scrutiny of stock issuance
4. Suspect background and experience of the board of directors
5. Neither widely held nor actively traded company stock

Apparent Inadequate Background and Experience of the Independent Auditor.   I was surprised that a Florida-based company with well over 100 training centers throughout the country would be audited by a sole practitioner based in a distant state. I grew increasingly concerned when it became evident that the audit involved numerous complications, including several stock offerings and acquisitions.

Questionable Accounting Policies Relating to Quality of Earnings. College Bound was able to show incredibly fast increases in both profits and assets—largely because of some questionable accounting policies: (1) capitalizing pre-opening costs as intangible assets, (2) declaring an insufficient reserve for uncollectible receivables, and (3) boosting profits through acquisitions using the controversial pooling-of-interest method.

Circumventing SEC Scrutiny of Stock Issuance. College Bound found several ways of issuing securities without the usual close SEC scrutiny. First, College Bound used a circuitous route to go public, merging into an existing shell public corporation, thus avoiding the usual close SEC scrutiny. Then, when College Bound wished to raise additional capital, it issued convertible notes in a private placement (outside the SEC's jurisdiction); the notes were subsequently converted into stock.

Suspect Background and Experience of the Board of Directors. A board of directors should serve two important functions: (1) augment the management team in those areas in which it is deficient, and (2) independently oversee and evaluate management to protect the shareholders' interests. Unfortunately, College Bound's board failed on both counts: Board members, as a group, had little apparent expertise in running a fast-growing service business; furthermore, they were clearly not independent with respect to College Bound.

Neither Widely Held nor Actively Traded Company Stock. One risk common to shareholders of closely held businesses is liquidity risk—the inability to sell their shares at a moment's notice. Because most shares were held by insiders at College Bound and relatively few shares were traded, investors clearly had such a liquidity risk.

Epilogue. Shortly after my article was published in January 1992, College Bound's stock price started drifting downward from $22 per share. A bombshell was dropped during the week of April 6, when the SEC filed a motion in U.S. District Court alleging possible fraudulent financial reporting and requesting that College Bound immediately turn over certain documents.

Although the company maintained its innocence, the stock price plummeted from \$17 to \$7 in just one week, including a $5\frac{3}{4}$-point decline on a single day. One week later College Bound suffered another severe setback, when the SEC suspended its stock for 10 days. The third, and fatal, blow occurred on April 23, when the SEC sued the company, alleging that College Bound had defrauded investors by churning bank accounts to "massively" inflate revenues. Within hours of the court filing, College Bound's founders, George and Janet Ronkin, resigned their positions as chief executive officer and president, respectively. On April 29, College Bound filed for bankruptcy.

Understanding the Basics of Financial Reporting

Overview

This tutorial provides the basic tools for reading and interpreting financial statements. Specifically, it describes the following:

- Basic accounting principles and journal entries
- The structure and purpose of each major financial statement
- Key aspects in understanding financial statements

Financial statements summarize economic transactions and measure profitability and financial condition. Companies that use financial shenanigans distort actual profits (or net income) and financial condition.

Accounting Is as Simple as 1-2-3

Some of you may have never taken an accounting course. Others may have taken a course or two, yet remember nothing. In either case, it doesn't matter—because in the next few pages you will learn all the formal accounting you need to know to understand financial statements. All you need to remember are three lessons.

Lesson No. 1

Accounting is really quite simple, since *all* transactions fit into one basic equation:

$$\text{Assets} = \text{Liabilities} + \text{Capital}$$

In nontechnical terms, the equation states that the total book value of the resources (owned by the entity) are equal to the book value of the claims against those resources.

Assets represent economic resources—cash, inventory, buildings—that will provide future benefits beyond the current year.

Liabilities represent claims against those resources by creditors, vendors, employees, and others.

Capital represents the residual claim against those resources by the owners (shareholders).

The balance sheet is the formal financial statement that shows the details of a company's assets, liabilities, and capital.

Lesson No. 2

One major component of capital is a company's profits for the current year. Profit (or net income) is computed as follows:

$$\text{Net income} = \text{Revenue} - \text{Expenses}$$

Revenues (or sales) are the inflows of net assets (i.e., assets less liabilities) from selling goods or providing services.

Expenses are the resources consumed in the process of generating revenue.

Net income, a measure of operating performance, is calculated as the excess of revenue earned from selling a product or providing a service above the efforts required or expended to sell the product or provide the service.

Thus, whenever a company records revenue, both net income and capital increase. Conversely, whenever a company records an expense, both net income and capital decrease.

The statement of operations (or income) is the formal statement that shows the details of a company's revenues and expenses.

Lesson No. 3

For the equation, Assets = Liabilities + Capital, to hold, there must be at least two parts to each and every transaction. For example, when an asset account increases, another asset account must decrease; a liability account must increase; or owners' equity (i.e., capital) must rise.

That's all there is to it. Everything else (as they say in the Talmud) is just commentary.

Applying the Lessons

All information shown on financial statements is first recorded in a series of journal entries. Let's examine some common business transactions and their effect on the accounting equation (A=L+C) and on net income.

Checklist: Guiding Principles

1. Revenue should be recorded after the earnings process has been completed and an exchange has occurred. Similarly, gains should be recorded when there is an exchange.

2. An enterprise should capitalize costs incurred that produce a future benefit and expense those that produce no such benefit.

3. As an enterprise realizes the benefit from using an asset, the asset or a part thereof should be written off as an expense of the period.

4. When there is a sudden and substantial impairment in an asset's value, the asset should be written off immediately and in its entirety, rather than gradually over time.

5. An enterprise has incurred a liability if it is obligated to make future sacrifices.

6. Revenue should be recorded in the period in which it is earned.

7. Expenses should be charged against income in the period in which the benefit is received.

Transaction No. 1: Sale of Merchandise

Increase:	Accounts Receivable	500		(asset)
Increase:	Sales		500	(revenue)

Whenever a sale is recorded, assets, revenue, net income, and capital all increase. The accounting entry usually is made when a sale has taken place and the merchandise has been shipped out. If a company records revenue too early (Shenanigan No. 1, as discussed in Chapter 3,) or creates fictitious revenue (Shenanigan No. 2, as discussed in Chapter 4), net income, assets, and capital have been overstated.

Transaction No. 2: Receiving Cash When Future Services Are Due

Increase:	Cash	200		(asset)
Increase:	Unearned Revenue		200	(liability)

This transaction increases assets and liabilities. One accounting trick (Shenanigan No. 5, Chapter 7) is to record revenue instead of unearned revenue. The result is that net income and capital are overstated and the liabilities are understated.

Transaction No. 3: Receiving Cash at Time of Sale

Increase:	Cash	900		(asset)
Increase:	Sales		900	(revenue)

This transaction increases assets and revenue. One accounting trick used when a company wants to defer some sales revenue until a later period is to record a liability initially and wait until the following year to transfer the liability to revenue. This trick, also known as setting up reserves (Shenanigan No. 6, Chapter 8), shifts income from a year in which a company may have a large profit to a later year when profits are weak. The objective is to "smooth" income over the years, eliminating the peaks and valleys.

The journal entries to set up and later tap a reserve are as follows.

This year's entry:

Increase:	Cash	600		(asset)
Increase:	Unearned Revenue		600	(liability)

Future year's entry:

Decrease:	Unearned revenue	200		(liability)
Increase:	Sales Revenue		200	(revenue)

The result is that this year's sales revenue is recorded as earned in a later period.

Transaction No. 4: Estimating Probable Liability

Increase:	Loss from Litigation	6,000		(loss)
Increase:	Estimated liability		6,000	(liability)

This transaction increases liabilities and reduces net income. One accounting trick (Shenanigan No. 5, Chapter 7,) is neglecting to record this entry. The result would be that liabilities are understated and net income overstated.

Transaction No. 5: Recording the Purchase of an Asset

Increase:	Equipment	10,000		(asset)
Decrease:	Cash		10,000	(asset)

This entry exchanges one asset for another. One accounting trick (Shenanigan No. 4, Chapter 6) is to record this entry when a company acquires an expense (a past benefit) rather than an asset. For instance, a company pays an advertising bill and decides to record advertising as an asset. The proper entry for recording an expense is:

Increase:	Advertising Expense	500		(expense)
Decrease:	Cash		500	(asset)

By recording an asset ("capitalizing") rather than an expense, the current period's net income will be overstated. As the equipment is used over the next several years, however, the cost will be transferred from the asset account to depreciation expense. Thus the net result of incorrectly capitalizing an expense is that the expense is improperly shifted from the current period to a later period.

Transaction No. 6: Amortizing an Asset

Increase:	Depreciation expense	500		(expense)
Decrease:	Equipment		500	(asset)

This entry transfers a portion of the asset to an expense as the benefit is received. A company purchases various assets to use in producing its product and in generating revenue. When revenue is recognized (as a sale takes place), that portion of the assets that can be associated ("matched") with the sale should be transferred from the assets to expenses. One accounting trick (Shenanigan No. 4, Chapter 6) is transferring those assets too slowly to expense, either by amortizing over too long a period or by failing to write off worthless assets. The result of either error is to record too small an expense and thereby to shift expenses to a later period.

Alternatively, if a company is concerned that profits in the later periods will be inadequate, a strategy may be to set up reserves. As indicated earlier (Shenanigan No. 6, Chapter 8), one way to set up reserves is to shift revenue to a later period. Another approach (Shenanigan No. 7, Chapter 9) is to shift future-period expenses into the current period. Simply depreciating a larger amount this year and smaller amounts in future years would give you those desired results. Another way to shift expenses to the current period is by prepaying next year's expenses.

Transaction No. 7: Recording
Gain on Sale of Assets

Increase:	Cash	15,000		(asset)
Decrease:	Equipment		10,000	(asset)
Increase:	Gain on Sale		5,000	(revenue)

Recording a gain on the sale of assets boosts assets and net income. One accounting trick (Shenanigan No. 3, Chapter 5) is to sell off assets, especially those with low book values, and record a gain on disposal.

Structure of Financial Reports

Economic performance is generally communicated to interested parties in the form of financial statements. These reports include: (1) the statement of income; (2) the balance sheet; and (3) the statement of cash flows.

The Statement of Income

The statement of income (also called the statement of operations) illustrates the profitability of a company for a specified period of time. A company's profit or net income is equal to its revenues and gains minus its expenses and losses.

The following is the Gillette Company's statement of income. (*Note:* The Gillette Company is used for illustrative purposes only, and *not because it committed any shenanigans.*)

Notice that there are several important subclassifications within the statement of income:

1. *Gross profit* (or gross margin, when stated as a percentage of revenues): excess net sales over cost of sales

The Gillette Company
Statement of Income

| | 1990 | | 1989 | |
	Dollars	Percent Sales	Dollars	Percent Sales
Net sales	4,344.6	100.0	3,818.5	100.0
Cost of sales	1,824.6	42.0	1,581.9	41.2
Gross profit	2,520.0	58.0	2,236.6	58.8
Operating expenses	1,747.3	40.2	1,572.5	41.2
Operating income	772.7	17.8	664.1	17.6
Nonoperating items	−179.5	−4.2	−190.5	−5.2
Pretax income	593.2	13.6	473.6	12.4
Income tax	225.3	5.1	188.9	4.9
Net income	367.9	8.5	284.7	7.5
Earnings per share	$1.60		$1.35	

2. *Operating income* (or profit from operations): gross profit less operating expenses, such as selling, general, and administrative

3. *Income from continuing operations:* net income after taxes, but before any noncontinuing transactions (such as extraordinary gains or losses, the effects of a change in accounting principles, and gains or losses related to discontinued operations)

4. *Net income* (net income after tax, or NIAT) (or net margin, when stated as a percentage of revenue): income from continuing operations plus or minus the noncontinuing transactions

Note: Since The Gillette Company had no noncontinuing transactions during 1990 or 1989, its income from continuing operations is the same as its net income.

The Balance Sheet

The balance sheet (or statement of financial position) presents a *snapshot* at a specific point in time of a company's resources (i.e., its assets) and claims against those resources (i.e., its liabilities and owners' equity or capital). The asset portion of the balance sheet reports the effects of all of a company's past investment decisions. The liabilities and owners' equity portion reports the effects of all of the company's past financing decisions. Capital is obtained from both short- and long-term creditors and from owners. Thus the balance sheet reflects the following equation:

$$\text{Assets} = \text{Liabilities} + \text{Owners' Equity}$$

That is, the book value of a firm's assets or resources equals the book value of the claims against those assets by creditors and owners.

The balance sheet for The Gillette Company is shown on page 176.

Uses of the Balance Sheet.   An analyst, voicing frustration in using a balance sheet to analyze a company, stated: "A balance sheet is very much like a bikini. What it reveals is interesting, what it conceals is vital." Many others have been left asking what vital information is found beyond the numbers. Is the company hiding any material information?

While the task of interpreting a balance sheet might be daunting, those who have mastered this skill often find important insights concerning problems on the horizon. One such expert, Michael Murphy, editor of the *Overpriced Stock Service* newsletter, believes that "the potential problems of technology companies always show up first on the balance sheet."

The balance sheet provides information about the present resource base and how those resources were financed. It provides useful information on management's stewardship of invested capital and about the solvency and liquidity of a company. A review of the liabilities and owners' capital reveals the financial commitments of a company and the relative interests of the owners and creditors. Such information may have a bearing on a company's financial strength (ability to meet its long-term obligations) and its financial flexibility.

By examining the current assets and current liabilities, analysts can judge a company's liquidity (ability to meet its short-term obligations). Current assets minus current liabilities is called "working capital." It is viewed as a measure of financial safety—a cushion against uncertain drains of financial resources in the future.

Limitations of the Balance Sheet.   The balance sheet *does not* indicate the current value (or "market value") of a company's

The Gillette Company
Balance Sheet

	1990 Dollars	1990 Percent Assets	1989 Dollars	1989 Percent Assets
Assets				
Current assets:				
Cash and equivalents	81.2	2.2	136.8	4.4
Receivables	1,015.7	27.7	828.5	26.6
Inventory	758.4	20.7	688.2	22.1
Prepaid and other	238.2	6.6	201.0	6.5
Total current assets	2,093.5	57.0	1,854.5	59.6
Plant assets	1,986.1	54.1	1,680.5	54.0
−Accumulated depreciation	1,124.5	−30.6	935.7	−30.0
Net plant assets	861.6	23.5	744.8	24.0
Intangible assets	240.2	6.5	260.4	8.2
Other assets	476.0	13.0	254.3	8.2
Total assets	3,671.3	100.0	3,114.0	100.0

Liabilities and Equity (Capital)				
Liabilities				
Current liabilities	1,307.9	35.6	1,061.3	34.1
Long-term debt	1,045.7	28.5	1,041.0	33.4
Minority interest	334.9	9.1	259.2	8.3
Deferred taxes	117.4	3.2	82.5	2.6
Total liabilities	2,805.9	76.4	2,444.0	78.5
Equity				
Capital stock	838.1	22.8	737.7	23.7
Additional capital	176.8	4.8	169.4	5.4
Retained earnings	1,635.6	44.6	1,430.0	45.9
Currency translation	−209.5	−5.7	−183.9	−5.9
Treasury stock	−1,575.6	−42.9	−1,483.2	−47.6
Total equity	865.4	23.6	670.0	21.5
Total liabilities and equity	3,671.3	100.0	3,114.0	100.0

assets, liabilities, or owners' equity. Instead, it presents the "book value" (or "historical cost") of all these items.

Second, some elements of value of a business *may never appear* on the balance sheet because they cannot be expressed in dollars.

A brand name that has attracted customer loyalty (such as Coca Cola), and an industry reputation for quality products are examples of "unrecorded assets."

A third limitation is that the balance sheet *represents only one moment in time*. Seasonal factors and unusual circumstances must be considered. Even when comparative balance sheets for several years are presented, they fail to explain *why* changes occurred, particularly those related to operations. Accordingly, the statement of income and the statement of cash flows are essential complements to the balance sheet.

The Statement of Cash Flows

The statement of cash flows reports the net cash (inflows minus outflows) from the three principal business activities—operating, investing, and financing. An example is given in the table on page 178.

As shown in The Gillette Company example, there are three major sections on the statement of cash flows: (1) cash from operations, (2) cash used in investment activities, and (3) cash used in financing activities.

One key question addressed on the statement of cash flows is whether the company generates enough cash from operations by itself or must generate cash from investments (e.g., by selling off assets) and/or from financing (e.g., by issuing debt or equity issues) to meet its cash needs.

Key Aspects of Understanding Financial Statements

Analysis of financial statements focuses on four main characteristics:

- Profitability
- Liquidity
- Solvency
- Activity (or operational efficiency)

The Gillette Company
Statement of Cash Flows

	1990	1989
Cash from operations:		
Net income	367.9	284.7
Depreciation	117.0	149.1
Other	21.1	53.1
Working capital	−118.1	−145.4
Total from operation	447.9	341.5
Cash from investing:		
Additions to property	−255.2	−222.6
Sale of property	25.5	8.1
Acquisition of businesses	−113.6	−72.3
Sale of businesses	122.1	—
Other	27.3	−24.1
Total from investments	−193.9	−310.9
Cash from financing:		
Issuance of preferred stock	100.0	600.0
Purchase of treasury stock	—	—
Proceeds—stock options	7.8	5.1
Proceeds—long-term debt	31.0	27.6
Reduction of debt	−196.8	−649.7
Change—loans payable	−59.4	71.2
Dividends paid	−159.2	−113.9
Total from financing	−276.6	−59.7
Exchange rate effect	−6.4	−17.8
Net increase (decrease)	−29.0	−46.9
Cash at beginning	109.5	156.4
Cash at end	80.5	109.5

Profitability Ratios

Profitability ratios measure the financial performance of a company over a period of time. There are a number of profitability ratios which analysts commonly use, including: (1) gross profit margin, (2) operating margin, (3) net profit margin, (4) return on assets, (5) return on equity, (6) earnings per share, and (7) price/earnings ratio. Using the financial statements of The Gillette Company, these ratios are described as follows.

Profitability Ratios

Gross profit margin	= Gross profit/sales
Operating margin	= Operating profit/sales
Net profit margin	= Net income after tax (NIAT)/sales
Return on assets (ROA)	= NIAT/total assets
Return on equity (ROE)	= NIAT/total equity
Earnings per share (EPS)	= NIAT/number of common shares outstanding
Price/earnings (PE) ratio	= Price per share of stock/EPS

The Gillette Company
Profitability Ratio

	1990	1989
Gross profit	58.0	58.8
Operating margin	17.8	17.6
Net margin	8.5	7.5
ROA	10.0	9.1
EPS	$1.6	$1.35
PE Ratio	22.0	25.0

Gross Profit Margin (or Gross Margin) = Gross Profit/ Sales. Gross profit margin measures the margin available to cover a company's operating expenses and yield a profit.

Operating Margin = Operating Profit/Sales. Operating margin measures a company's profitability from its main source of business.

Net Profit Margin (or Net Margin or Return on Sales) = NIAT/Sales. Net profit margin measures how much a company earns for each dollar of sales. Thus if a company has a net profit margin of 3%, it earns three cents on every dollar of sales.

Ten Highest Returns on Sales—1990

1.	De Beers Consolidated Mines	34.4%
2.	Whitbread	29.9
3.	Petronas	26.2
4.	Glaxo Holdings	26.1
5.	Merck	22.8
6.	Guinness	21.7
7.	Eli Lilly	21.7
8.	Codelco-Chile	18.6
9.	SmithKline Beecham	17.9
10.	American Home Products	17.8
	The S&P 500 Median	3.3

SOURCE: *Fortune*, July 29, 1991.

Return on Assets (ROA) = NIAT/Total Assets. Return on assets measures the return on investment of both the stockholders and creditors.

Ten Highest Returns on Assets—1990

1.	Lyondell Petrochemical	25.9%
2.	Merck	22.2
3.	American Home Products	21.8
4.	SmithKline Beecham	20.7
5.	Iscor	19.4
6.	Bristol-Myers Squibb	19.0
7.	Sasol	18.4
8.	Abbott Laboratories	17.4
9.	Petroleos De Venezuela	17.2
10.	Glaxo Holdings	17.0
	The S&P 500 Median	3.4

SOURCE: *Fortune*, July 29, 1991.

Earnings per Share (EPS) = NIAT/Number of Common Shares Outstanding. Earnings per share measures the profitability of the company accruing to common stockholders on a per-share basis.

Return on Equity (ROE) = NIAT/Total Equity. Return on equity measures the return on investment for the stockholders.

Ten Highest Returns on Owners'
Equity—1990

1.	Lyondell Petrochemical	936.8%
2.	Gillette	138.6
3.	FMC	103.8
4.	SmithKline	102.0
5.	Ralston Purina	67.7
6.	KOC Holdings	57.9
7.	Avon Products	49.6
8.	General Mills	47.1
9.	Merck	46.5
10.	American Home Products	46.0
	The S&P Median	10.8

SOURCE: *Fortune*, July 29, 1991.

Price/Earnings Ratio (or PE ratio) = Price per Share of Stock/EPS. The price/earnings ratio measures the stock market's current valuation of the company as related to the company's recent earnings. A low price/earnings ratio may indicate that a company is conservatively valued; alternatively, a high ratio might indicate an overvalued company.

Liquidity Ratios

Liquidity ratios indicate the amount of cash or short-term assets (such as receivables and inventory) available to the company. If the liquidity position gets too high, then the company is sacrificing profitability; if the liquidity position gets too low, then the company may not be able to meet its current obligations. Some key liquidity ratios are as follows.

Liquidity Ratios

Current ratio = Current assets/current liabilities

Working capital = Current assets − current liabilities

Quick ratio = (Current assets − inventory)/current liabilities

Inventory to net = Inventory/(current assets − current
working capital   liabilities)

The Gillette Company
Liquidity Ratios

	1990	1989
Current ratio	1.60	1.75
Working capital (in millions)	$785.60	$793.20
Quick ratio	0.84	0.91
Inventory to working capital	0.97	0.87

Current Ratio = Current Assets/Current Liabilities. The
current ratio measures the extent to which the claims of the short-
term creditors are covered by the company's current or short-
term assets.

Working Capital = Current Assets − Current Liabilities.
Working capital measures the excess of current resources over the
current obligations. The greater the working capital, the greater is
the cushion to meet any unforeseen cash requirements.

**Quick Ratio = (Current Assets − Inventory)/Current
Liabilities.** The quick ratio measures the extent to which the
claims of short-term creditors are covered without the need for an
inventory sell-off.

**Inventory to Net Working Capital = Inventory/(Current
Assets − Current Liabilities).** Inventory to net working capital measures the extent to which the company's working capital
is tied up in inventory.

Solvency Ratios

Solvency (leverage) ratios, which reflect a company's ability to
meet its obligations, indicate how the company finances its operations. If a company's leverage (debt) is too high, then it may be
taking great risks; if it is too low, then it may be failing to take

advantage of opportunities to use long-term debt to finance growth. Some examples of solvency ratios are as follows.

Solvency Ratios

Debt to assets	= Total debt/total assets
Debt to equity	= Total debt/total equity
Long-term debt to equity	= Long-term debt/total equity
Interest coverage ratio	= Operating income/interest expense

Debt to Assets = Total Debt/Total Assets. Debt to assets 𝑥 measures the extent to which a company borrows money to finance its operations.

Debt to Equity = Total Debt/Total Equity. Debt to equity measures the creditor's funds as a percentage of stockholders' funds.

Long-Term Debt to Equity = Long-Term Debt/Total Equity. Long-term debt to equity measures the balance between a company's debt and its equity; a high financial leverage indicates a risk in meeting the principal and/or interest on the debt.

The Gillette Company
Solvency Ratios

	1990	1989
Debt to assets	0.76	0.79
Debt to equity	3.24	3.65
Long-term debt to equity	1.21	1.55
Interest coverage	4.57	4.55

Interest Coverage Ratio = Operating Income/Interest Expense. The interest coverage ratio is calculated from the income statement. It measures the multiple by which the operating income exceeds the fixed interest expense which must be paid. The higher the ratio, the less chance of defaulting on the payment.

Call Debt Issuers & find out Min. Ratios.

Activity Ratios

Activity ratios indicate the productive efficiency of the company. Generally, stronger activity ratios are associated with higher profitability (due to high productive efficiency). Some examples of activity ratios are as follows.

Activity Ratios

Inventory turnover   =   Cost of sales/average inventory

Accounts receivable =   Sales/average accounts receivable
turnover

The Gillette Company
Activity Ratios

	1990	1989
Inventory turnover	2.52	2.36
Receivable turnover	4.71	4.90
Days turnover	77.50	74.50

Inventory Turnover = Cost of Sales/Average Inventory. Inventory turnover measures the number of times a company turns over all its inventory during a year. The higher the turnover, the shorter the time that a company must sit with idle inventory.

Accounts Receivable Turnover = Sales/Average Accounts Receivable.   Accounts receivable turnover measures the number of times a company turns over all its receivables during a year. The higher the turnover, the more quickly customers are paying their bills.

Using the Ratios

Ratios are used to compare a company's current performance to its prior years' performance and to the performance of similar companies in the industry. Information about these ratios can be obtained from the following sources, among others:

- *Almanac of Business and Industrial Financial Ratios* (Prentice Hall)

- *Annual Statement Studies* (Robert Morris Associates)
- *Dun's Review* (Dun & Bradstreet)

Limitations of Using Ratios

Financial ratios must be used with caution for the following reasons.

- These ratios are merely "surrogates" for an underlying measure, such as liquidity or solvency; they should therefore be recognized as imprecise measures.
- If management is manipulating the numbers on the financial statements, then the resulting ratios will necessarily also be misleading.
- Ratios consider only information that is quantified on the financial statements. Excluded, yet often equally important, are qualitative and quantitative information that is not shown on these statements.

Other Books of Interest on Financial Shenanigans

Adam, James Ring, and Douglas Frantz. *A Full Service Bank*. New York: Pocket Books, 1992.

Dirks, Raymond L., and Leonard Gross. *The Great Wall Street Scandal*. New York: McGraw-Hill, 1974.

Mayer, Martin. *The Greatest Ever Bank Robbery*. New York: Charles Scribner & Sons, 1990.

Miller, Norman, C. *The Great Salad Oil Swindle*. New York: Cowan McCann, 1965.

O'glove, Thornton. *Quality of Earnings: The Investor's Guide to How Much Money a Company Is Really Making*. New York: The Free Press, 1987.

Potts, Mark. *Dirty Money*. New York: National Press Books, 1992.

Seidler, Lee J., Frederick Andrews, and Mark J. Epstein. *The Equity Funding Papers*. New York: John Wiley, 1977.

Soble, Ronald L., and Robert E. Dallos. *The Impossible Dream: The Equity Funding Story*. New York: Putnam, 1975.

Staley, Kathryn F. *When Stocks Crash Nicely: The Finer Art of Short Selling*. New York: Harper-Business, 1991.

Sternberg, William, and Matthew C. Harrison. *Feeding Frenzy*. New York: Henry Holt and Company, 1989.

Waldman, Michael. *Who Robbed America?* New York: Random House, 1990.

Index

About the Author

Howard M. Schilit is a leading authority on detecting accounting tricks that cause financial statements to be misleading. As a result of his pioneering work in uncovering financial scams, he has been quoted in *The Wall Street Journal*, *The New York Times*, *Business Week*, *Forbes*, and numerous other publications. On two occasions he has been featured in Louis Rukeyser's nationally syndicated column. His "shenanigan busters" seminar is popular among investors, lenders, auditors, and others. A professor of accounting at American University, Schilit is the coauthor (with W. Keith Schilit) of *Blue Chips and Hot Tips* (1992).